MAKING
MINUTES
MATTER

Your Guide To Being Content
With How You Spend Your Time

Mary Kutheis

Making Minutes Matter
Your Guide To Being Content With How You Spend Your Time
Mary Kutheis

Published by Fountain Pen Press, St. Louis, MO
Copyright ©2019 Mary Kutheis

Editor: Maria Rodgers-O'Rourke

Cover and Interior design: Davis Creative, DavisCreative.com

Publisher's Cataloging-In-Publication Data
(Prepared by The Donohue Group, Inc.)

Names: Kutheis, Mary, author.

Title: Making minutes matter : your guide to being content with how you spend your time / Mary Kutheis.

Description: St. Louis, MO : Fountain Pen Press, [2019]

Identifiers: ISBN 9781732848405 (paperback) | ISBN 9781732848412 (ebook)

Subjects: LCSH: Time management. | Executives--Time management. | Stress management. | Contentment. | BISAC: SELF-HELP / Self-Management / Time Management. | SELF-HELP / Self-Management / Stress Management. | SELF-HELP / Personal Growth / Happiness.

Classification: LCC HD69.T54 K88 2019 (print) | LCC HD69.T54 (ebook) | DDC 650.1/1--dc23

2019

ATTENTION CORPORATIONS, UNIVERSITIES, COLLEGES AND PROFESSIONAL ORGANIZATIONS: Quantity discounts are available on bulk purchases of this book for educational, gift purposes, or as premiums for increasing magazine subscriptions or renewals. Special books or book excerpts can also be created to fit specific needs. For information, please contact Fountain Pen Press, mary@mckcoaching.com.

For M.O.M. and Dad.
I miss you every day.

TABLE OF CONTENTS

Introduction

If it seems like every year time is going faster, it's because it is. Maybe not literally, but it does feel that way. Here's why the feeling is so palpable.

When you were four years old a year was one quarter of your entire life! But now, you're older. I'm 57 so a year is 1/57th of my life! That's a much smaller piece of the pie that is your time on this earth.

If you feel like time is going a little too quickly for your comfort and you want to make the most of every day, you're reading the right book.

I talk with business people every week who are tired. Some are overwhelmed with the sheer volume of things they need to get done personally and professionally. Their To-do lists are never-ending and feelings of accomplishment are few. Mostly because for everything that gets crossed off, three new tasks get added.

From the moment they hit their desk chair in the morning they go non-stop. Sometimes accomplishing what they set out to do but not as often as they'd like. Every day is a blur of busy-ness and yet the results they experience don't indicate the progress they want.

Leaving the office at the end of the day often feels like an escape rather than a thoughtful wrap up to the day.

Work is often taken home to be done with some resentment or ignored accompanied by guilt.

1

Falling into bed at night, exhausted, thoughts turn to what didn't get done and how quickly another day is going to dump more responsibilities in their lap.

If this sounds familiar—a lot or even a little—stick around. Because it doesn't have to be this way. Many, many people who had these same feeling are looking at life and work very differently today because they did the things you'll read in this book.

In this book you'll find little or no fluff. I tried to keep it simple because that's how I like things. A short story here, a quick example there, is all I added in order to help concepts make sense. You're busy enough as it is. If it wasn't critical to the content, I left it out to save you time.

You'll find no secrets and no tricks. People call ideas and tips "secrets" and "tricks" to catch your attention and that doesn't feel authentic to me. By definition, secrets aren't meant to be shared. You'll find straight talk and real-world solutions that work.

I'm not promising you that this book will fix your time management challenges once and for all. That statement is hype and not my style. Life is constantly changing and evolving. You go through busier and less busy eras that need to be noticed, assessed and adapted to.

You will, however get foundational strategies that can impact the rest of your life in ways you may not have imagined. I can confidently say that because it happened for me and for the many people who have gone on this path before you.

What you will also find is relief from overwhelm and something refreshingly positive to replace the feeling that your efforts never seem to be enough.

Are you ready? Then let's get going before another minute passes.

CHAPTER ONE

Ready to Take Back Control

My Story

It was 2015 and I sat at the kitchen counter with tears welling up in my eyes. The feeling wasn't remarkable because I was slowly falling apart in the days leading up to this day.

My business at the time could not be described as successful and had been on that track for more than two years. I had some clients and a little revenue but was constantly in fear of not being able to pay the company bills that came in every month. Bills I was incurring because I kept trying tactics to help me be successful. I built a new website. Hired a coach to help me brand myself and figure out what I should say on sales calls. I joined a group to help me with accountability, so I would actually make those calls. All of those strategies cost me money and none of them solved my not-enough-revenue problem.

The tears came from frustration as much as from fear. I knew I had a very important message to share with people struggling with overwhelm, but I wasn't sharing it. And I wasn't getting any closer to figuring out why.

But let me back up.

I started my business in 2001 and built it steadily over the years. In 2012 I lost my biggest client. I had done a very dumb thing in allowing just one client to be the majority of my income. I knew it was a bad idea and a lousy way to run a business, but I let it happen.

I didn't actually lose my biggest client. I resigned my biggest client.

At first, spending almost all of my time with this one company was a joy because they were different than any other company I'd seen. It was so refreshing! I ditched corporate America to start my own business because I was so fed up with the dysfunction where I worked.

So, I had this wonderful client that changed the paradigm I'd experienced. As much as I liked the work I was doing with this innovative organization, I knew I should start filling the pipeline again and onboarding new clients.

But before I could make enough progress, the bottom fell out. The company started changing. Changing so dramatically that I could no longer continue the work I had been doing with any integrity. Though I didn't realize this at the time, they were no longer aligned with my core values, so I had to go.

In Chapter Four we'll talk more about Core Values. Knowing what yours are is vital in order to make good decisions about how you spend your time. When I defined mine, it became clear why I'd made decisions that sent me in good—or not so good—directions.

This dream client that started off in such a positive and promising way shifted into dysfunction so quickly and completely, that my heart was broken. I truly believed they were different. When I realized that they would not be the exception I had so trusted they would be, I calmly and professionally removed myself from the equation.

I resigned them as a client and promptly reduced my revenue by about 80%.

I needed to get back out there and market myself as a coach, trainer and speaker. My mission up to that time had been to share the importance of being productive. "Don't waste time. Work smart not hard." Blah blah blah. As a Productivity Coach I had built up a book of business before and knew I could do it again.

Except that I wasn't doing what I needed to do to attract new prospects and clients. I felt weirdly paralyzed.

Frustrated with myself, I started talking to smart people I hoped could help me figure out my problem.

I spoke with several successful international authors, trainers and speakers. While serving as the programming chair of our local chapter of the National Speakers Association, I had the great fortune to spend time around these brilliant and generous people when they came in town to present programs for our chapter.

I spoke to a former coach and mentor who it seemed always knew exactly where he was headed. He was then and is now a tremendous success helping clients and companies boost business performance.

I spoke to other friends and colleagues with businesses similar to mine. They could immediately relate to my challenges and also helped me sort through the mishmash in my head.

I journaled, meditated, ruminated and mind mapped random thoughts and ideas.

Finally, I went through an exercise to determine my core values.

All of those activities served to uncover the truth of my dilemma:

I didn't care one whit about productivity.

There I was, out there calling myself a Productivity Coach and yet productivity meant nothing to me. My disinterest was clearly the thing that was holding me back from reaching out to market and sell productivity training. Primarily, because being authentic was and is one of my core values.

Telling everyone to get more productive when I didn't care about productivity was about as inauthentic as it gets.

But what *did* I care about?

The answer that kept showing up was this.

"I want people to be content with how they spend their time."

Note: The word "content"—accent on the second syllable—hits some people in a very negative way. If you're one of those people, I'm asking you to reserve judgment until you read Chapter Two.

That was it. The words felt as comfortable as well-worn jeans. I knew that was what I wanted to help people do.

But while my mission became clearer back then, it wasn't a smoothly paved road to get from there to here.

Because no one I was aware of was focused on that message, there was no road map. For many people that wouldn't be a problem. They would just start creating the road themselves. But that wasn't me.

I had been a rule follower my entire life. I wanted people to tell me the rules so I could follow them.

To that end I spent countless hours and dollars on sales training, train the trainer training, marketing consulting, website development training, PR training, training to be a better speaker, you name it. Each time what I wanted was for the expert to tell me the *right* way to do things.

In fact, each one of them probably did. They advised, coached or trained me on the method that worked for them. But unfortunately, those same methods weren't always what I really needed.

I was in uncharted territory for what I wanted to share. When I firmly decided that "contentment" was the word that defined my message, I got LOTS of pushback. "Well that's fine and all but no one is going to buy that." "You have to stick with the 'money' word, which is productivity." "No company is going to hire you to help their employees be content. They want them to be productive."

While I wanted to shout my message about the importance of being content with how you use your time, I didn't have the gumption to go all in. I tiptoed around sharing that idea. I would mention it, but water it down to keep people from dismissing me entirely. The rule follower in me said, "What if you are wrong?"

I believed in contentment at my core, but to avoid risk, my public focus remained productivity.

And my revenue continued to be dribs and drabs of what it could have been. The worst part of that wasn't the lack of money, it was the people I wasn't helping. Overwhelmed, stressed people who really needed this message and this information.

Too afraid to show my real message and too unmoved to actually talk about productivity, the only thing I managed to do authentically, was cry.

Until I got mad. At myself.

When that happened, I decided to throw out the rule book and go my own way with my own message. And that is what got me here, writing this book for you.

I help people, specifically you, be content with how you spend your time.

Though my commitment to *sharing* the importance of contentment is only four years old, the ideas have been percolating for decades. I spent 17 years in corporate America—where I learned what doesn't work. For the last 19 years I've been developing and honing ideas to help smart, ambitious people like you feel good about how you spend your time. In this book I share with you what I've shared with hundreds of clients.

How you spend your time is key to living a contented life.

If you want that contentment, let's get started.

If you don't like your current results...

The very first concept I created in my business was this...

If you don't like the results you're getting you have two options: **Change what you do and get different results; Or, change how feel about your current results.**

This book is built around that concept. In these pages you'll find ideas for new ways to do things and new ways to think. Here's what we're going to cover:

For the rest of this chapter I'll share some foundational information and ideas to set the stage for the work that follows in Chapters Two through Eight.

In Chapter Two, a deep dive into the idea of Contentment. If you're already on board, you'll get revved up to do the work that follows. If you're skeptical about the idea of contentment as a worthy state of mind, you'll get enough information to see if you can kick that skepticism to the curb.

Next, a chapter on each of the two most important skills you will need as you try valiantly to successfully accomplish what you want to achieve despite the crazy busy pace of the world. One chapter is devoted to getting skilled at Choosing. That's followed by a chapter centered on honing your ability to Focus. The ability to Choose and the ability to Focus are cornerstone skills in the effort to use your time wisely. When you use your time wisely, you'll naturally be more content with your life.

Then we'll focus on Processes. The real-world, step-by-step plans you need to streamline your efforts.

If you've ever procrastinated about anything (I know no one who hasn't), the chapter on Procrastination is for you. Tons of insight and ideas beyond what you may have already run across.

Finally, we close the book talking about your physical and mental self—and how to make the most of both.

You Must be Ready to Try

"You have to at least try it. One bite."

Ever hear that as a kid when a pile of beets was staring at you from the dinner plate? You protested that you didn't want to eat it because, "I hate beets and they will make me vomit!"

"But," your mom countered, "you've never HAD beets so how could you *know* that?"

"One bite. Then you can leave the table." The standoff begins.

I work with clients who want to change something about their life at work. They might be overwhelmed by too much to do and not enough time to do it, not organized enough, procrastinate—robbing them of peace of mind, have trouble delegating or priori-tizing, wish everyone could just get along, need to have a difficult conversation, etc.

In order to make these changes, I work with them to learn additional skills, develop better processes, create new systems, encourage changes in mindset, etc. And occasionally, that's where the standoff can begin.

I work with smart, successful people who are, more often than not, lifelong learners. They regularly seek to improve their own skills and mindset and consequently have usually tried a lot of things with greater or lesser degrees of success.

Change can be hard—especially if something about the new idea seems either familiar or too "out there." Routines can be so, well, routine, they can seem impossible to change even though they're not working as well as they might.

"I tried that and it didn't work," or "That won't work for me," or "I'm not going to do that," they sometimes say or imply. In fairness, I don't expect my clients to take orders—we're equals after all—and push-back is not only welcomed but encouraged.

At the same time, being unwilling to even *try* a new way prevents them—and you—from experiencing the change we all seek.

Back to the beets. It's possible that the first bite *is* vomit-inducing and now, unpleasantly, you and stern parent both know.

This actually happened in my family. My sister despised corn relish and I'll bet my Dad wished he had listened to her when she said the outcome would be ugly if she was required to eat it. After leaving the restaurant, Dad was at the wheel with sister standing behind him in the back seat. (No seatbelts in the 1960s.) He ended up wearing the corn relish down his back. "Told ya!"

But it's also possible that the first bite just gives you data about small changes you need to make so you will like it. I despise beets but love borscht. Go figure.

Likewise, when you attempt to change behaviors or your mindset, the first step may not be comfortable. You will need to step out of your comfort zone. You have to do it in order to see where to go next. Always be honest with yourself about how much you are trying to apply the solutions.

When you have a solution in front of you, give it a fair shot and see where it works and where it doesn't. Make changes from there and you're on the road to better results.

EXERCISE

Think of something you've learned that had the potential to help but you never gave it enough of your effort to see if it would work. It may be a practice to reduce your stress or a way to manage meetings. Just about any idea you may have picked up in a book or article but never got any further than reading it and saying, "Hmm. That sounds interesting." This time, grab a notepad, jot it down, and take some steps to try it.

No Promises This Will Be Easy

When was the last time you felt triumphant about something you achieved or accomplished? What was it? If you were asked, "What about achieving it was so rewarding and made you so happy?" what would you answer?

Here's a story about effort, reward and happiness.

A colleague shared a story about bonuses that were given out at his company. Some departments were high performers and succeeded well beyond their stated goals while others didn't even meet the minimum requirement. To determine bonuses, all the quality and customer satisfaction scores were combined, and everyone got the same bonus percentage.

My colleague said you could tell, just by the demeanor of the employee, into which category they fell. The high performers were happy and proud of the job they had done and had animated chats about the bonus. The sub-par performers were subdued and didn't discuss the addition to their paycheck.

Interesting. You might think the high performers would be upset that they didn't get a bigger bonus because they actually put forth greater effort. Or that the under-performers would be thrilled they received a bonus at all.

Back to your feeling of triumph I asked about. Why did it feel so great?

The most common reason people give is because success *didn't* come easy.

In my colleague's company, the high-performing workers were happy because they *worked* for it. The under-performers were less happy because they knew, deep down, they hadn't earned it.

Isn't that the case for you? You were elated about your success because you worked for it. Perhaps you even overcame some big obstacles or fears. Your effort got you the result you wanted.

Even in tough times, the joy isn't all about the money. It's about persevering in spite of it being a grind. People love to tell "war" stories about the all-nighter they pulled to meet the client's demand, or the eating plan they stuck to in order to drop that last 10 pounds, or how they gave a winning presentation when they used to be terrified to speak in front of people.

Accomplishment against the odds feels great. Working hard feels great. Giving in to fear and procrastination feels lousy. Making excuses feels even worse.

Books that promise easy fixes or gurus that offer over-the-top results with minimum effort are feeding you a load of garbage. Don't eat it.

If you're struggling with overcoming procrastination or getting your schedule under control or knowing what to do when, it may not be easy to get things the way you want them to be. But, boy will it be worth it.

Three Good Options

Speaking of changing things up, always remember these three options:

Do it differently–change your process

Delegate it–get someone else to do it

Dump it–Just stop doing it or having it done altogether

You may be surprised at how many things can end up in these categories, leaving you with more time in your day and your life.

In the chapters that follow you'll get information to help you decide which of those options is best for you and solid ideas about how to put the best option into action.

What I Learned from People Like You

In a survey, I asked several questions about what the respondents were struggling with the most. I'll share those results with you in a minute, but for now, I'd like to ask you the same questions.

Each question is framed as an ideal state or condition. For instance, "I have a clear plan for each day and for the majority of the time I am able to follow that plan." Each question has five possible answers indicating the amount of time this ideal state is your reality.

For each question use the scale below and write next to it the number that corresponds with your experience:

5–All the time

4–Most of the time

3–Half of the time

2–Less than half of the time

1 – Never

1. I have, and use, an efficient and effective process for handling email.

2. I am NOT significantly impacted by interruptions during the workday.
3. I consistently do the most important tasks first, rather than doing the easy tasks first.
4. I'm able to focus when necessary and do not feel the need to multitask.
5. I am content with how I spend my time, both personally and professionally, and maintain what I consider to be a good work/life balance or blend.
6. I have a clear plan for each day and for the majority of the time am able to follow that plan.

For any question you answered that you live in this ideal state half of the time or less, there's room for improvement. If you feel like you're in that ideal state most or all the time, it doesn't need immediate, or any, attention.

Now, you can see how your responses measure up to the other respondents. For each question I've provided two numbers. The top figure represents the percentage of responses being in the ideal state more than half the time. The bottom figure represents the percentage of responses indicating being in the ideal state half of the time or less. The questions are listed in order from most to least challenging situation—based on responses.

1. I have, and use, an efficient and effective process for handling email.
   More than half of the time–19%
   Half of the time or less–81%
2. I am NOT significantly impacted by interruptions during the workday.

More than half of the time–25%

Half of the time or less–75%

3. I consistently do the most important tasks first, rather than doing the easy tasks first.

More than half of the time–29%

Half of the time or less–71%

4. I'm able to focus when necessary and do not feel the need to multitask.

More than half of the time–29%

Half of the time or less–71%

5. I am content with how I spend my time, both personally and professionally, and maintain what I consider to be a good work/life balance or blend.

More than half of the time–38%

Half of the time or less–62%

6. I have a clear plan for each day and for the majority of the time am able to follow that plan.

More than half of the time–42%

Half of the time or less–58%

These responses show that while these challenges aren't universal, they're quite common. If you find yourself in the bottom half today, you're in the right place and you're certainly not alone.

Work your way through this book and make some key changes. Soon you'll find yourself purposefully rising to the top.

Start Thinking in Terms of "Worklife"

It's unlikely you've heard the term "worklife" yet. Why? Because I made it up. The work I do with my clients is focused primarily on time at work. But we're not business robots. We have a life at work. Work is part of your life and it's a big part. Big enough that it deserves focused attention on how to make time spent there a good as it can be. So, I call it your "worklife."

Know that as you read the ideas here they've been developed as a response to challenges experienced at work. However, the skills learned and mindsets achieved are sure to positively impact your personal life as well.

You're not a different person at work and at home. The challenges you face at work impact your time away from work. If you're going through a rough patch personally, it's impossible to shut that out entirely just because you're on the job. If your job is frantic, boring or overwhelming, you'll bring that same energy back home with you. When you're content with how you spend your time at work, you'll be more content with how you spend your time all the way around.

Why Other Solutions Haven't Worked

Chances are this isn't the first book you've picked up on time management. Perhaps you've even taken a webinar or workshop on how to get a better handle on your time. But you're here, so you must still want some help. If you didn't get the result you were looking for with those other options, you wouldn't be the first. Here are several reasons why it may not have turned out the way you hoped.

The Solution was Too Complex

Over the years, I've coached people who latched onto a new system only to give up in frustration days—or hours—later. Why? The system was too complex.

There are systems out there that have flowcharts that make my eyes cross. Are you supposed to run every decision about every task through a giant flowchart? How much time will that take? Time that could be spent actually accomplishing something!

There are color-coded systems and special notebooks or planners to capture and prioritize your tasks. There are dozens if not hundreds of software platforms and apps you can use as stand-alone task management systems or as add-ons to other systems. For many, electronic solutions create a hurdle that ends up being a dead end. More about that later.

If you have to spend days or weeks just to learn or understand the approach before you can use it, it's too complex for you.

You're seeking solutions because you don't have enough time as it is. If the solution makes your life more complicated, how can that be a good thing?

Life is complicated enough. The ideas in this book are simple. Candidly, you may have heard variations of some ideas before, but I've worked hard to pare the strategies and processes down to bare bones. Working through the ideas and exercises IS a commitment, but it's do-able.

The Change was Too Drastic

You may have been asked to change too much at one time or just entirely too much.

The best changes work with your current habits and preferences. Changes need to be small, purposeful and cumulative.

I coach with clients for sixteen weeks for a reason. Change needs to happen incrementally in order to stick. 180's never work long-term.

Change something. Try it for a bit. Adjust. Practice it for a bit longer. Add another small change to the new process. And so on.

Patience, grasshopper. Even Olympic swimmers get better in fractions of seconds. As small as the improvements are, those fractions can make the difference between being *on* the podium or looking *at* the podium.

The changes you make along the way may sometimes seem insignificant, but they're not. Every single one matters.

The "If I can, you can too" Theory

You've seen stories about the newly fit man who lost 100 pounds and finished a marathon. Or the woman who goes from living in her car to being a multimillionaire in business. Because their earlier lifestyle was so wildly opposite of the current state, they claim that if they "Can do it, ANYONE can."

Bull. Crap.

To be absolutely certain you can accomplish the very same achievement, all the factors about that person and their experience would need to be the same for you and your experience. You would need to have access to the same resources, motivation, support, desire, level of intelligence, commitment, opportunities, economy. You get the drift.

There are over 30,000 books on time management out there and another 50,000-plus on productivity. The reason there are so many is that the ideas in any one of them work for some number of people. At the very least, the ideas work for the person who wrote the book.

The ideas I put forth in this book will work for many, many people, but if you have circumstances, other than your own willpower, that prevent you from achieving success, you could still struggle.

I'm not a naturally organized person. I've just learned over time that I function better if things are simple and orderly, so I've built systems and routines to support that. If you thrive on chaos, this isn't the book for you.

People may have similar challenges, but the solutions are nuanced because everyone isn't the same. Change is individual. This book gives simple, followable advice that will work for lots of people. If you think it should work for you but it doesn't, get in touch with me and we'll see what might be going wrong. I'm serious. Call or email me. We'll talk.

The 21 Days to a New Habit Myth

Just about everyone interested in self-development has heard the theory that it takes 21 days to create a new habit. Personally, I had never had success making that happen. So, I tried to research how others were doing it and what I was missing.

Have you ever been perplexed like I was, and thought, "Why am I the only one who hasn't been able to make this 21-day miracle stick?"

Turns out we aren't the only ones. No one else is doing it, either. Further, there's no science to back up the idea. But I can tell you where this myth got started:

Psycho-Cybernetics by Maxwell Maltz. I happened to pull that book from my shelf one day to give it a re-read. It had been years since I picked it up and I thought I'd give it a skim.

And there it was.

The passage explains that should the reader attempt the ideas in the book, he shouldn't get discouraged if change doesn't happen right away.

"Instead, reserve judgment—and go on practicing—for a minimum period of 21 days."

"It usually requires a minimum of about 21 days to effect any perceptible change in a mental image. Following plastic surgery, it takes about 21 days for the average patient to get used to his new face...People must live in a new house for about three weeks before it begins to 'seem like home.' These and other commonly observed phenomena tend to show that it requires a minimum of 21 days for an old mental image to dissolve and a new one to jell."

He's talking about an *image* not a *behavior*. Big difference!

Evidently, over the decades this idea has morphed into the idea that you can develop a new habit in 21 days.

Nope. Not so.

What you *can* do is develop a new routine that will start to feel more familiar within a few weeks.

A routine is not a habit—and the distinction is critically important.

I talk in detail about routines in Chapter Six and as part of that discussion, a bit about habits. For now, if your routines eventually become habits, great. But when they don't, you still have the routine established and can use your brainpower for more important things than re-inventing processes for repetitive tasks.

Tactics, Motivation and Desire

When you're struggling with time management, you may fall into one of two camps:

1. You don't know what to do to better manage your time; or,
2. You *know* what to do to better manage time but still aren't doing it.

These two key areas of challenge mean you lack the tactics, have motivation issues, or simply don't have a strong enough desire tied to the motivation. All of these are powerful, and frankly critical, when it comes to getting better results.

Let's take one at a time.

Tactics

This is for people who really have little or no idea how to manage a busy work schedule, prioritize effectively, get organized, stay focused, get things done, use time wisely, etc. If that's you, you'll get what you need here. In the coming chapters I'll share tactics for:

- Improving your ability to choose
- Increasing your ability to focus
- Developing efficient and effective processes
- Overcoming procrastination

These tactics are the tools you need to overcome your time management challenges. Tactics may be all you need. Or you may need to look at the quality of your motivation and desire.

Motivation and Desire

My dad started smoking before I was born and kept it up every day of his life. As smoking became less and less socially acceptable he had more pressure to give it up. He couldn't smoke inside homes other than his own. Many public places had begun banning smoking. The cost of cigarettes continued to climb. Perfect strangers would "inform" him of the dangers to his health.

As far as motivation to quit, he had plenty. It would save his health, fatten his wallet, get him welcomed back into homes and restaurants. So, he went through auricular therapy in an effort to quit. That's not a typo. Auricular therapy is where the external surface of the ear is stimulated to alleviate a condition in another part of the body. In this case, as a smoking cessation method.

It worked. He no longer craved cigarettes.

He was utterly miserable.

You see, there were all sorts of *motivations* to quit smoking. Trouble was he had no *desire* to quit.

Smoking wasn't just sucking on lit tobacco for him. It was relaxation. It was social time. He missed it terribly. It was the weirdest thing. He didn't *have* to smoke anymore because of addiction, he *wanted* to smoke because he enjoyed his life with cigarettes in it.

It's a perfect example of motivation not being enough to make a change. Here is another:

A gentleman hired me to help him figure out how he could stop working on Saturdays and still get everything done.

When coaching a client, I'm purposeful in uncovering the motivation and desire before we start looking at new tactics.

His motivation was clear. His wife really hated that he worked on Saturdays. She wanted him to spend time with the family and on some Saturdays even take over childcare entirely. As a stay-at-home mom she needed a break.

So how about his desire? He had zip, zilch, nada desire to give up his Saturday workdays. Turns out he loved working on Saturdays because he could get so much done when the office was quiet. When we figured that out, our strategy shifted.

The solution wasn't to stop working on Saturdays, it was to look at his entire schedule and see where he could fit in more family time and ways to let his wife get a breather. We were able to examine how he managed his workload and shift enough activities to meet both of their needs and desires.

Your Motivation

The motivation to use your time wisely may include having more quality time with family, more time to relax, being able to make more money without working more hours or having time to focus on getting healthier.

EXERCISE

Why are *you* motivated to make changes? Take a few minutes and really think about it. Write down as many reasons as pop into your head. You'll need that information to take the next step.

What are my motivations to make these changes?

For the record, I'm not a big fan of motivational quotes and don't even get me started on those sappy motivational posters. Quotes and posters mean nothing if you don't take action. And action requires desire. Which is where we go next.

Your Desire

Now that you know you know your motivations, are they accompanied by desire? Do you really *want* more time with your family? Some folks with seriously dysfunctional families don't.

Do you *like* relaxing or would you just be bored?

Do you want more money or just think you *should* because people will see you as more successful?

Will you exercise and pay more attention to nutrition when you have more time? Or in truth, are you happier that you don't have time to spend your energy that way?

Look at each one of your motivations and assess your level of desire. Without desire, you won't have enough oomph to do what you need to do to make change. Since you already feel pressed for time, don't waste any of it reaching for things you don't really want.

EXERCISE
Specifically, what desires would be fulfilled by making the changes I'm considering?

I Understand You

I'm not a psychologist or mental health professional. But I do have keen insight into human behavior. Through experience, intuition, training, and tools, I understand why we behave the way we do and how you may be standing in your own way. Work through this book, pick up the ideas and tips that serve you, and in the end you'll be smack dab in the middle of having more contentment in your life.

CHAPTER TWO

Mindset Shifts

State of Mind Model™

As a result of working with hundreds of businesspeople, I've created the State of Mind Model. It's a set of behaviors I've witnessed to greater or lesser degrees in the workplace.

On the bottom half of the model are Panic, Anxiety and Complacence.

Panic is the feeling you get when you've overslept for an important meeting, the client moves up the deadline by several days, you realize you're coming in over budget, or a punitive boss ominously calls you into her office.

It's also a feeling some people seek. Some people thrive on the thrill panic creates. Like riding a roller coaster. You're terrified as the car crawls up the incline and then momentarily feel sick to your stomach as the car crests the peak and starts to plummet.

But quickly, exhilaration hits. And that can be intoxicating. People who say they do their best work when they wait until the last minute, are very often people who love the rush that comes with panic.

Anxiety is next. Where panic can sometimes be exciting, anxiety is living under a dark cloud, waiting for the other shoe to drop. Anxiety is worry—or like a yoga instructor once said, "Praying for what you don't want."

Complacence is giving up. Phoning it in. In a literal sense, the slacker would be too complacent to actually pick up a phone. These are folks who have decided that effort and caring won't do any good. Maybe they are this close to retirement or work in a company culture that is so dysfunctional they see no need to work at making it better or do decent work.

But be warned: The one thing complacent people aren't complacent about is complaining. And their toxicity can bring down a team, a department or an entire small company.

Contentment is in the middle on the top half of the scale. And you'll note that it's nestled right above Complacence. The placement is purposeful because the two are not the same thing and it's vital to have that fact front and center.

Contentment is feeling good about the choices you make about how you spend your time. It's feeling good about what you've gotten done, even though it may not include everything on your to-do list. It's feeling upbeat about taking steps toward getting that big new client, even if the contract isn't yet signed. It's patting yourself on the back for making good food choices at points throughout the day, even if there were a few "less good" choices made, too. With the right mindset you have opportunities for many—even dozens—of moments of contentment in a day.

We'll talk more about contentment later.

Striving is seeking more. More happiness, more money, more clients, more success, more fitness, more love, more opportunities, more skills, more intelligence, more vacation, more dessert. More. And there's not a thing wrong with that. But it must not be at the expense of being content with what you have or what you've done *right now*.

Joy is at the top of the scale. Joy is what you feel when you see your first child or grandchild (or niece, nephew, etc.), or land that big client, or finish the half-marathon, or step out of the airport terminal at the start of your vacation and get hit with that balmy breeze or complete the tedious project. Joy doesn't come about every day, but when it does, you revel in it.

EXERCISE

Take a few minutes and look into your own experiences. Can you identify times when you were in each State of Mind?

What was happening? Who was involved? How did that State of Mind affect your day or week?

You want to spend as little time as possible at the bottom of the scale and as much time as possible at the top. Contentment, Striving and Joy combined equal Happiness. Your happiness resides in the top half of the scale.

Striving is easy. You do that every day, often without thinking. Joy is wonderful and yet less frequent. But Contentment—That's something within your power to feel every day. Even many times a day!

The best part? The choice is yours.

More About Contentment

Passive. Complacent. Resting on your laurels. Unambitious. Mediocre.

Those are words some people believe are synonymous with being "content." That somehow being content is settling for less than you might achieve.

I get push-back from well-meaning colleagues, friends and random people who believe promoting contentment is worthy of an eye-roll. Many feel that contentment is for lazy people who settle for mediocre.

That thinking is *so* wrong.

Contentment is the absence of panic, anxiety and complacence. It's the feeling you can have every single day, comfortable with the actions you've taken and the choices you've made. It is the peaceful place of accomplishment that rejuvenates you, inspires you and prepares you for what's next.

A sense of peaceful happiness is the *definition* of contentment.

Therein lies the reason that contentment is exactly the right word, at exactly the right time, for anyone who wants to have success in life *and* be fulfilled and happy. The very idea that people are uncomfortable with the word "content" means they have forgotten (if they ever knew) what it means and how to experience it.

In Flow: The Psychology of Optimal Experience by Mihaly Csikszentmihalyi, the book jacket adds, "Steps to Enhancing the Quality of Life." This says best what the book is about. Many authors and scholars consider this work an instructive, profound resource contributing enormous insights into human behavior and our desire for happiness and fulfillment.

This passage appears early in the book:

"In fact, there is no inherent problem in our desire to escalate our goals, as long as we enjoy the struggle along the way. The problem arises when people are so fixated on what they want to achieve that they cease to derive pleasure from the present. When that happens, they forfeit their chance at contentment."

That is the sadness, or worse, the tragedy! That we spend our lives always striving and never taking those moments to recognize and celebrate our achievements, regardless how small. All it takes is a moment of awareness that you have taken a step forward—no matter that the step isn't across the finish line. Moments of contentment are what make life rich and contribute to happiness and a sense of peace.

So how can somebody say that "contentment" is for slackers? You can't. Contentment is for the wise ones who know that a life well-lived is one where "enjoying the struggle" is even more important than what lies ahead. There's plenty of time to enjoy the future—just wait until it becomes the present.

Further evidence that complacence and contentment aren't synonymous is that you cannot be content if you're not giving it your best. Giving it your best is exactly the opposite of complacence.

It's important to note that giving it "your" best may not be giving it "the" best. Your best is going to vary from day to day. Do the best you can and that's all you can ask.

You'll know if you've given your best. And you'll know when you haven't. Though when you haven't you still may be pretty good at convincing others that it was indeed your best. But you can't fool yourself. And you're the person that matters.

Do your best and know it to get those moments of contentment.

One other mindset can steal your contentment: Your best never being good enough. As Csikszentmihalyi says, if you are focused only on striving, you forfeit your chance at contentment. Stop the "never enough" thinking.

Feeling like nothing you do is ever enough is a lousy way to go through life. Experiencing contentment requires thinking in a new way and focusing more on progress rather than perfection.

If your goal is to increase your revenues by 10%, you don't have to wait until you get there to experience satisfaction and contentment. In fact, noting and taking time to revel in small achievements will make the process more rewarding.

If someone ever tells you that being content is for losers, we know who's really losing out.

Speaking of other people, as you set out to make some positive changes about how you spend your time, let's talk about the others in your life.

Others Stealing Your Contentment

Be careful about letting others steal, determine or affect your contentment. You see, there are a lot of people out there who while they might not like it, are more comfortable having reason to complain, than they would be if everything was going well for them. Those people may have a difficult time witnessing your effort to feel contentment. Seeing you feeling good just makes them feel less-than. They prefer misery and misery loves company. They want you back, so you can be gloomy, bummed-out buds.

In many cases, you can just choose not to be around people like that. If it's someone you meet while networking or on social media, avoid them. If they're people you see infrequently, just smile as they dismiss, mock or criticize your efforts and make a speedy exit.

But sometimes these contentment road blockers are in your inner circle. Could be a boss or co-worker. Could be a friend, parent, sibling or spouse. Which makes it significantly harder to extract them from your life.

How this might look in practice: You've set a goal to get a new, more satisfying job. In most cases that's not an easy project and can take some time. You'll have days where you make good progress and other periods of time where your efforts seem to stall through no fault of your own. Maybe you even lose out on an opportunity you really wanted. You keep a positive outlook, know you're doing the best you can and have a sense of peace and contentment about that.

The negative person in your life decides that your contentment with your progress isn't warranted. They'll zero in on the fact that you haven't gotten a better job yet or that there is so much competition you'll never stand out. Or that making more money will just make you change for the worse because wealthy people are snobs.

That's when your internal strength is most important. You think this person who cares about you *should* be looking out for your best interest. Little bits of doubt creep in. You think perhaps he's right, and you're silly to measure success in the way that you do. "I must be doing something wrong if I still don't have the job I want. Maybe I'm not good enough after all." And there you are, back in the place of self-doubt and anxiety.

I've seen this happen where one partner is building a business and the other partner gives subtle cues to let him know she doesn't believe he can achieve that goal. It takes strength to believe in your success when someone close to you doubts it.

Other people can't take away your contentment unless you allow it. Contentment is all about what's inside, not what other people perceive. It's about how you view the choices you've made and the progress you've experienced.

Don't allow anyone else to control your moments of contentment.

Life Balance is BS

Have you, like me, had it up to your eyeballs with the term "work-life balance"?

Enough already.

For starters, the term itself is flawed. Work and life are not two opposite sides of the scale you're trying to balance. Work is part of life, not distinct from life. That's why I coined the term worklife.

Second, the idea of balance is overrated. Balance indicates an even-ness, an equality that's difficult, if not impossible to attain. For instance, you have a family situation that requires a great deal of your personal time. The scale is going to tip heavily to that side of your life and make you unbalanced—which feels very stressful if you feel pressured to immediately restore balance. Your priorities tell you to focus on family while the need for balance says get back to work. Aargh!

Personal and professional lives should blend—not balance.

Think of this potential to blend in terms of a color wheel. Say your individual personal life is red. The part of your personal life that includes friends and family is yellow. Those two areas frequently overlap, creating a vibrant orange. Red, yellow, orange. Three colors which are lovely, but also limiting.

Your professional life, on the other hand, is blue. Blue is pretty, but still, just blue.

However, when you blend red, yellow and blue you have every color imaginable available to you! There's no limit to what you can create when you take bits from each part of the color wheel and blend them to create new, vivid colors.

The idea of blending rather than balance is achievable, and more accurately describes how you live your life. You don't leave your personal life behind when you sit at your desk. Neither do you leave your professional life at work when you close up shop at the end of the day. A few behavioral changes aside, you are the same person at work and at home. For many people, work IS at home. You have the same preferences, challenges, dreams, and strengths regardless of where you are, physically and mentally, in a given moment.

According to Freelancers Union, one in three working Americans is an independent worker—and the number is growing. Independent workers—and even those employed by larger companies but who are also responsible for how they manage their time—must be able to shift from personal to professional and back again many times in a day.

It's a Personal Professional Fusion

What you call it matters because words have power. If you're expending vast amounts of energy trying to create work-life balance and not succeeding, it feels like failure. How can you fail at something that's unrealistic in the first place?

Look at the fusion of your personal and professional lives and assess whether what you're experiencing works for you. If not, make some changes. Not to achieve balance, but to experience the "colors" that motivate you, excite you and bring you success, peace and fulfillment.

Do you remember giving the balance beam a try in grade school P.E. class? Or perhaps trying to balance a basketball on the tip of your finger, like the Harlem Globetrotters?

Even when you got sure footing for a moment on the beam, or for an instant got the ball to stay on your finger, it wasn't the time to breathe a heavy sigh and relax. "Whew. Finally balanced for *good!*" No. A loud noise from across the gym could blow your concentration, sending you wobbling off the beam to the mat. A hiccup or a lightning-fast glance away from your finger would bring a quick end to the balanced ball.

What's so intriguing about achieving life balance, given that the very word connotes something tenuous and fleeting? Wouldn't you be better off to reach for a goal that doesn't require constant adjustments every second?

What about life *blending*? What about having a comfortable blend of personal fulfillment and professional success? What if you didn't look at your personal and professional lives as though they sit on opposite sides of an old-fashioned scale, requiring you to continually dart back and forth to keep the trays in balance?

I get tired just thinking about it, much less doing it.

If we're going to use the word balance, then it needs to be the balance a surfer has. The balance required to stay on the board comes from an internal source—her core. With a strong core the biggest waves don't knock her down, they give her an exhilarating ride into shore.

The work in this book will help you develop a figurative balanced core.

You know if you have a comfortable blend or not. If you work 15-hour days, sleep 6 hours a night and so have 3 total hours a day of personal time, that's certainly not balanced, but it may work just fine for you. If that's your story and it *doesn't* work, then re-mix the blend.

Life balance is an attention-grabbing buzz word (or two) and has been for some time. It's easy to get wrapped up in the hype and end up striving for something you neither need nor want.

Later in the book I'll be walking you through an eye-opening exercise that will show you how balanced or unbalanced your life may be. Armed with that information you'll have the tools to create the blend or fusion that makes you happier.

Your Brain Only Knows What You Tell It

Sticks and stones may break my bones, but words can never harm me.

To that I say, "What a *load*." Words have a *powerful* ability to cause harm.

Sadly, you can be pretty cruel sometimes. Not cruel to other people—to yourself.

"I'm such an idiot." "I'll never catch onto this." "I have no discipline." "I'll never stop procrastinating." "Boy that was a stupid thing to say." "I'm always late."

See what I mean? Looking at it in black and white, it's startling to see how we berate ourselves.

Talented, accomplished, smart, engaging, sometimes even award-winning people make themselves a punching bag for all the things they don't achieve.

Instead of counting the wins for the day, the focus is on what *didn't* happen. Sound familiar?

But research shows that beating yourself up is counterproductive. Pardon me if this sounds like you should beat yourself up for beating yourself up. The harder you are on yourself, the more difficult it is to get into the mindset that you can accomplish whatever you set out to do.

I went on a 30-day sugar fast and broke it twice. In the past I might have figured that since I messed up the 30-day effort by eating a piece of candy the entire plan may as well be ditched. But that's senseless. My habit *had* been to eat sugar every day. Sometimes several times a day. Eating sugar two days out of 30 counts as a win.

My own experience backs up the research about being better off not beating yourself up. There's a level of confidence that I can pass up the candy sitting on the counter any time I choose. "Heck, all of those other days passed with no sugar. Why not now?"

Have you ever tried to get your schedule under control or once and for all develop and consistently use a system to manage your tasks? You do well for a few days or weeks and then something happens to throw you off. The system that was working is now buried in a cluttered mind. You start overscheduling and noting tasks on scraps of paper like you used to do before you had the new system.

That's when the negative chatter can start and get you in trouble.

You tell yourself you'll never be able to stay on course and lo and behold you won't. Your brain doesn't want to make a liar out of you, so everything will line up to make you unproductive and unfocused.

Your brain only knows what you tell it.

When things get out of control tell your brain that you were doing just fine until the craziness hit. Reset and get back on track. All is not lost, it was just a small detour.

Focus on your wins, even if you consider them minor, and you'll have more of them. As a one-time "not enough-er", I understand if this will be tough mindset for you to shift.

This method might help, though.

Do you have children? If so, think of one of them at 3 or 6 or 13 years old. No children? Picture a kid you know and care about. Now imagine this child is standing right in front of you waiting to hear the next thing you're about to say. Ever, in a million years, would you tell that child he or she is:

- Always running late and therefore selfish?
- Hopelessly unorganized?
- Doomed to a low pay, unfulfilling job?
- An imposter?
- Horrible with money?
- Boring?

Of course not.

So, noodle on this. You were once that age. Today you're the same person essentially, just with a few more candles stuck in the frosting. Don't you deserve the same compassion, love and respect that you'd give to that child?

When you catch yourself saying such things, think about yourself as a kid and rephrase it to something more positive.

Be kind to yourself. Count the positives. Pat yourself on the back for the things you are, for what you have accomplished, for the incremental progress you've made.

I, for one, am cheering you on!

Nocebo Effect

You're likely familiar with the placebo effect. It's when a patient experiences a positive reaction to an inert drug or procedure because he has been told that's what the drug or procedure would do for him.

Not as well-known is the *nocebo reaction*. Coined by Walter Kennedy in 1961, it's essentially the opposite of the placebo effect. When patients were told that their prognosis was grim, their condition was more likely to worsen, despite interventions to make them better.

It's an example of the body following what the brain tells it to do or feel. The brain is remarkably powerful!

Think about what happens when you jump to a conclusion about how awful a meeting or project or task is going to be. The nocebo reaction kicks in and when you attend the meeting, dive into the project or start on the task, you're predisposed to look for negative experiences.

That negative disposition will seep into the work you're doing, limiting creativity, collaboration and energy. The nocebo reaction has ongoing negative ramifications for the health of your business and career.

Go into the exercises and ideas in this book with a positive, good-will-come-of-this mindset. If you're skeptical and pretty sure it's all hooey anyway, this isn't going to be a good use of your time.

Now that you know there's going to be some work involved in making the changes you want, is this the week for you to start?

Next Week Will Be Less Crazy

Think about your schedule last week. How was it? Pretty crazy? If it was, did you ever look toward this week and think, "Things will be more manageable next week. I just need to get through this one."

If you did, you've got lots of company. You see, most people when asked will say that though their current schedule is pretty jammed up and there's more to do than time do it, they believe next week will ease up a bit.

And then "next" week turns into "this" week and it's the same story. "Well this week turned out to be really intense after all, but I see a light at the end of the tunnel next week."

Right. That light is an oncoming bus filled with new deadlines, my friend.

For most people I know and all of my clients easy, light days are the exception. Easy weeks happen infrequently. And yet people still look at extreme busy-ness as the exception when it's actually the norm.

The problem is in unrealistic expectations. When you create the expectation that next week will be easier and it rarely if ever is, you set yourself up for disappointment.

If you do nothing differently, next week is going to be just as crazy as this week. Fortunately, this book is full of ideas to help you do things differently.

Ask "When?" Until You Can't Anymore

Think about your goals: An initiative you intend to tackle to grow your business or perhaps a self-development program you've been meaning to start. Could be coming up with a robust marketing plan, writing that book, losing 10 pounds, getting a better job, becoming more active in a social cause, etc.

Got one? Good.

Now, you need to be able to answer this one-word question: When?

When will you start? When will you work on it? When is your targeted deadline?

The first "When?" answer will likely be vague. "Soon," or "next week" or "tomorrow."

Ask the question again.

When?

This time, drill deeper. If your first answer was "next week," keep getting more specific until you've committed to a day and a time. You're not finished answering "When?" until you know exactly when you'll be starting/working on your chosen goal. Only then do you have any shot at accomplishing what you hope.

Broad plans are important because they're the map. But having a map doesn't get you there. *You* get you there. And knowing when you plan to arrive is the first piece of information you need in order to know when to start.

You need "whens" defined along the way to make sure your progress is on track. As I wrote this book, the start was defined by a meeting. The end was defined by a book-in-hand date. But I needed many "whens" in the process to meet interim commitments.

It's critical to look at your calendar and slot a defined "when." By doing so you're forced to look at how this project fits into what you're already committed to. You may even find that when you try to pinpoint a time "next week" there isn't any time available without making changes.

Defining "when" is a simple but not easy skill because you must commit yourself. Committing yourself to this means you're rejecting other ways you could use that time. Generally, people don't like to reject other options, so the cycle of starting at some vague future time perpetuates. Vague is the death knell for reaching goals.

Before you move onto something else, think again about that project or initiative you earmarked at the start of this section. I have to ask you...

When?

EXERCISE

Take a few minutes to jot some notes about a project you want to start and complete. Don't get bogged down in the detailed steps right now. Keep your commitments focused on a start date and an end date. Look carefully at your calendar and life to see how well this will fit.

When you've done your thinking, and if you've found that you do indeed have the capacity to add this project to your commitments, write the start and end dates on your calendar.

It's a great start.

Accomplishments Journal

One way to stay aware of the actions that can bring you contentment is to keep an Accomplishments Journal.

I'm a hit-and-miss journaler. Daily journaling of any kind has always felt overwhelming to me. This is one of those journals you don't have to stay on top of every day. "Journal when you want to or need to" is my motto.

Your Accomplishments Journal is a place to jot down things you accomplished. Anything at all. Little things count as much as the big ones. Seeing with your own eyes is hard evidence of your activity.

Have you ever had one of those insanely busy days where, despite your activity, none of your big stuff got done? You fall into your desk chair at 6:00 p.m. and say, "What did I even *do* all day?"

That's a perfect time to pick up your Accomplishments Journal and start writing down everything. Every call you made, email you wrote, fire you put out, dispute you mediated, etc.

Sometimes you'll have big, exciting things in your Accomplishments Journal. Many times, you'll accomplish a lot of big and little things and not even bother to put them in your Journal. The sole purpose of the Journal is to keep you from forgetting that you are indeed an accomplished person.

The act of writing down your accomplishments will help you. The act of going back and reading them when you're feeling a little despondent will be good for your soul.

The Secret of Life Is...

One of my favorite songs of all time is by James Taylor. It's called "Secret o' Life".

Listen to it sometime. These are my words, not his, but essentially, he says that the secret of life is being content with how you spend your time.

That's it. It's mind-blowingly simple and yet we can get so far off track without realizing it. In the hubbub of everyday living, busy-ness leaves us far afield from what drove us to be so busy to begin with. We just want to be happy.

Whether you're working or playing, striving or relaxing, in the middle of good times or less happy ones, if you can enjoy where you are in the moment, what happier goal is there?

In this book are ideas to help you achieve that.

CHAPTER THREE

Starting with A Solid Foundation

In the last chapter we talked about the myth that next week will be less crazy than this week. In this chapter you'll do an exercise that will give you a clear picture of what your weeks *really* look like.

The exercise is critical because in order to make changes you need to have a baseline—an accurate accounting of how you're spending your time now.

Extreme Productivity

I read an online article, maybe it was even an entire website, focused on Extreme Productivity.

I was NOT having it.

I've already shared with you that productivity in and of itself isn't all that important to me. So, it's probably not surprising that Extreme Productivity doesn't do much for me either.

Why be extreme? It sounds exhausting.

Reasonable works.

Let's dive in.

Reasonable Productivity

How do you keep pace with an ever-growing list of responsibilities, demands and interests? Being more organized is a goal for scads of people. Feeling the need to accomplish even more in the same amount of time, you buy how-to books (like this one) and planners and get on board with the latest app that promises the secret to maximum efficiency.

But what if you actually got that extra hour? What if there were 25 hours in every day? The things you could do with that extra hour! Relax, take up a hobby, exercise, read. The possibilities are endless! More on that notion later.

The Busy Executive

I once received a call from a busy executive looking for advice. In addition to her demanding career, she was a wife, a mother of three, actively served on a couple of charitable boards, was an avid golfer, and had recently begun the process of moving her elderly mother into an assisted living facility. She wanted to know how she could get it all done.

We both laughed that giving up sleep was her best option! Of course, that's not reasonable or advisable. So instead, we re-examined her expectations and priorities.

I asked many questions. What was really important to her? How much time did she spend in crisis mode? What was her planning process? How often did she feel focused vs. flustered? Whom did she have to delegate to? How did she decide on what she would focus her attention? In short order we gathered insights to guide our work. You'll gain those same insights for yourself throughout the book.

A Shift in Thinking

We began with the idea I shared with you in Chapter One: If you don't like the results you are getting, you have two options: Change what you are doing and get different results, or change how you feel about your current results. If having enough time to do everything is an issue for you (like it was for her), which do you choose? Change your behaviors...or change your expectations? Maybe both.

EXERCISE

Let's start by examining your day. For this exercise, you'll only need a pen, some paper, and your brain. First, draw a grid with eight boxes across and three boxes down. It should look like this:

Next, make two lists. The first list (List 1) is things that happen every single weekday without fail. For this exercise, use a workday rather than a weekend day. These things include working, sleeping, cooking/eating, personal grooming/getting dressed, driving to/ from work, spending time with children, etc. Go ahead and take a few minutes to do that exercise now.

The second list (List 2) includes things that happen randomly, but reasonably often. These include all kinds of errands (grocery, dry cleaner, gas station, shopping), as well as household chores, hobbies, leisure activities, social events with friends, family responsibilities, volunteer work, education, watching TV, managing finances/paying bills, vacations, time on the computer, etc.

Now grab both the 24-block grid you made and List 1. If sleep is on List 1—and it had better be—mark off the number of boxes that represent how many hours you sleep. Seven hours? Seven boxes. The next big chunk is probably work. If you work eight hours a day, mark off eight boxes. Do you spend time driving to and from work? Calculate how much time you spend in transit and mark off those boxes. How about preparing food and eating? On average, how long does that take on a given day? Mark those boxes off. Continue marking off boxes until you have accounted for every bit of time spent on List 1 activities.

Your Results

How many empty boxes do you have remaining? I've seen many people who didn't have any left! Remember, each box represents an hour, so if you have 22 boxes filled in, 22 hours of each workday are committed to daily, non-negotiable tasks.

Look at your empty boxes and look at List 2. Reasonably, is there enough time left in your day to accomplish everything on List 2? Of course, you can't forget weekends, and you've got quite a few hours there to get some things done. But also consider whether you want to spend all of your hours handling tasks. Do you want time to be spontaneous? Or to relax doing absolutely nothing?

Expectation Miscalculation

If, prior to doing this chart, you were under the impression you should be able to get everything on both lists done all the time, you were suffering from an "Expectation Miscalculation." In your mind, you miscalculate the amount of time you actually have, and consequently create unreasonable expectations. And when you fail to meet those expectations, you're frustrated, stressed and unfulfilled.

Note: If you have plenty of boxes left after your List 1 exercise, it's likely that someone close to you has a very different result. Keep in mind that others may be overwhelmed even though you are not. Compassion is recommended!

When Did Life Get So Crazy?

You might be thinking that at some point your life did seem manageable. How did this happen? Your life is like watching children grow. When you live with a child every day, the changes they go through hardly seem noticeable. But to the uncle who sees the child once a year, the changes are enormous!

Such is your life. Because you live from day-to-day, it's easy to not notice when new, often big, commitments get added to an already full life. You readily take on these new challenges, but because they crept in, it's not top-of-mind to consider off-loading some responsibilities.

If you look back at your life by decades, you can no doubt see dramatic differences between life in your 20s, 30s, 40s, 50s and beyond. But did you notice those differences as you were living them, or did the changes happen so benignly that they slipped into your daily routine without making an obvious ripple?

Armed to Make Changes

In order to know how much it's reasonable for you to fit into your schedule, you need to regularly take an inventory of your life and your responsibilities. What still fits? What's non-negotiable? What might need to be tabled until other things run their course?

Back to that extra hour I mentioned. My guess is that getting one more hour a day would be like making a few more dollars a year. At first, it's exciting. More money to spend as you please! But it doesn't take long for the extra cash to be absorbed into new bills to pay or spent on things you never knew you wanted or needed before.

I remember making $10,500 annually my first year out of college. I wondered how in the world I would ever spend all that money! Well, you know how this story goes. Not only was I able to spend it all, but as my income increased over the years, so did expenses.

Sure, having 25 hours a day would be great for a while. But soon it would start to seem normal and all 25 hours would be jam-packed with things to do. Then you'd want 26 hours a day.

This exercise shows in black and white that you probably can't do everything you've traditionally thought you could. What is the skill you need in order to better manage reality?

Choosing is the first of two skills you must have in order to successfully navigate a very busy life, which we will cover in Chapter Four.

For now, do you know what the opposite of choosing wisely is? Multitasking.

When it seems too difficult to choose between two things you need to do, you consciously or unconsciously try to do more than one thing at a time.

Let's talk more about that.

Multitasking

For several decades, nearly every job description has included "the ability to multitask" as a required skill. Consequently, it ends up on every resumè, too. As the world has sped up it seems multitasking is just required. You have to either be good at it—or say you're good at it—in order to measure up.

The problem is you can't. And you shouldn't.

If you've read anything at all about being productive or managing time in the last ten years, you've read articles about what a bad idea multitasking is. Perhaps the people writing job descriptions haven't read those articles yet.

Multitasking erodes the quality of your work. It isn't more time efficient. It takes longer to do two things at one time than it would to do each of them alone, because you have to keep shifting your brain from one task to the next and that shift takes time. All that shifting makes you feel scattered. A scattered brain leads to panic, anxiety, and overwhelm. The list of ugly consequences goes on.

Here is what you *do* need to be able to do: manage multiple projects, which is not the same as multitasking. We'll talk more about that later. But for now, it's time to practice.

Practice Not Multitasking

Practice not multitasking so you can get more comfortable with the feeling of focusing on one thing at a time. Pick something simple that you tend to multitask when doing and just do that one thing. Some examples:

- If you read email while you're on the phone, just talk on the phone.
- If you work on your laptop while you're watching TV, just work on your laptop.
- If you look at your smartphone while your child or significant other is talking to you, just focus on the person.
- If you watch TV while making dinner, just focus on making dinner.
- If you get on the phone while you're walking the dog, just walk the dog.
- If you flip through a magazine while watching a movie at home, just watch the movie.

You'll find it challenging to stop doing two things at once. It's going to feel slow, awkward and less productive. But once that feeling passes—and it may take many practice sessions to get there—you'll replace it with a more centered and calm mindset.

EXERCISE
Right now, choose one or two activities that you will single-task while doing. Write them here:

1. _____

2. _____

Now practice doing one thing at a time. Your session might be no more than 5 minutes! You don't have to dive into the deep end.

When you practice, jot down how you feel at the beginning of the practice session and how you feel at the end of the practice session. Keep track of any shifts in your demeanor—or contentment—as you get better and better at focusing on one thing at a time.

In life, it's common to change tasks a lot. The idea is that if you have ten tasks that take a minute or two a piece, just do them consecutively instead of concurrently. If you make a call and leave a message, that counts as a completed task and you can move onto some other task while you wait for a return call.

Remember, multitasking is the opposite of choosing.

Prioritizing

Multitasking is what happens when you don't choose—and choosing is the most important element of prioritizing. Prioritizing is simply choosing what's most important and/or in what order you'll do things.

You can't prioritize if you don't choose, and because choosing seems so daunting the default behavior is multitasking. See how it all wraps up in a potentially jumbled mess if you don't prevent it?

At a task level, you need a system to help you prioritize, and I'll be sharing that with you in Chapter Six.

You also need to be able to comfortably prioritize at a life level. How you spend your minutes is how you spend your life. How you spend your minutes affects how content you are with how you spend your lifetime. Being purposeful about your use of time just makes sense.

Having Clarity, Not Regret

In late 2014 and early 2015 my family situations, particularly the health of my mom, consumed most of my attention. On many occasions there was a choice to make about whether family, work, friends, volunteer commitments or personal time was the top priority. Especially in the last couple of months of my mom's life, anytime she was in the mix, she came first. I didn't have to make a decision. She was first. The clarity brought some peace at a very difficult time.

My business revenue took a big hit, but I didn't care. I knew I could go back and make money again, but when she was gone, there would be no do-overs.

As hard as it was to build my business back up, I have not once regretted my decision. That's the power of knowing and acting on your priorities.

It's your choice, too. I recognize that not everyone can do what I did. I have a very supportive husband who took up a lot of slack and never questioned my choice, even though it affected our family income.

You have to make decisions that work for you and your life. Getting clarity about that is key. The work we do in Chapter Four will uncover the information you need to make the right choices for you.

Priorities Shift

If you look at every category of things that can rise to the top of your priorities, you'll see that none of them have the priority every minute of every day. You may say family comes first, but does it really? All of the time?

I'd step in front of a train for my son but even with that being true, business or other priorities often come before him. He doesn't need me 100% of the time. If I have a client commitment and he's hungry for lunch, he's on his own. He's 19 for heaven's sake! If I have a client commitment and he's been rushed to the hospital, he wins.

Sometimes friends or relaxation comes first. At least they should come first sometimes. It's about timing.

For some, work comes first no matter what. While I understand that, it's not for me. Is it for you? Or can you put work first during certain segments of your day and lower down the priority list other times of the day or week?

Be skilled at prioritizing for both tasks and life situations and you'll be at peace with how you're spending your time.

Chapter Four is all about solidly identifying your priorities in life. With that information, you'll know what's right for you and choose what to do based on that.

When we get into Processes in Chapter Six, you'll learn a simple system to prioritize your tasks. And as I've said before, your tasks are how you spend your minutes, and your minutes are how you spend your life.

Planning

Being spontaneous is creative, adventurous and fun, right? Planning everything is for rule-followers, rigid thinkers and sticks-in-the-mud. Nobody wants to be defined that way!

Many proudly spontaneous folks bristle at the idea of planning. They think that only uptight, Type-A sorts plan everything out and that doing so stifles creativity.

Yeah, well. They're wrong about that.

Imagine this.

You're going on vacation but haven't settled on a destination.

Should you fill up the car with gas or make airline reservations? Hard to say. Depends on where you're going.

Should you pack swimsuits or sweaters? Who knows—depends on the weather at your destination.

Can you make it a long weekend? Or should you plan on a week or more? Tough to determine that until you know how much time you'll be spending getting to and from your destination.

It's impossible to get to your destination and be prepared—if you don't know where you're going.

Business is like that, too. One reason people don't reach their business goals is that they don't know what their goals are and therefore can't take the right steps to get there.

You can spend every day in a flurry of business activity and yet still not get any closer to your destination, because you're not really certain what your destination is.

Because you're so busy, you feel like you just have to dive in and get stuff done. There are so many things screaming at you from your to-do list that rather than taking time to plan, it feels better to just start checking things off the list.

The problem with working without a plan is that you tend to do the easiest items first instead of the most important. Peak energy is spent tackling top-of-mind tasks first and by the time you get to the tasks that may be more important and/or more challenging, the best part of the day is used up. Willpower and brainpower have flagged and that makes doing the hard stuff even harder.

The answer is taking time to plan your day before you do anything else. No matter how busy you are, take just ten minutes to look at your schedule for the day along with your to-do list and carve out time to handle your most pressing tasks.

Be aware of when you are at your sharpest and plan your day then. As an example, I'm raring to go early and have less mental energy at the end of the day. So, I plan my day in the morning. Some people are bleary-eyed in the morning but fired up and productive in the afternoon. Those people would do better to plan later in the day for the following day. For late afternoon or close-of-day planners, the following morning will be more productive because you made decisions when you were clear-headed. Now, all you have to do is follow your own plan. No decision making required before your coffee has taken effect.

If you're tempted to say you don't have time to plan no matter what the time of day, look at it this way: Do you spend even ten minutes doing any of these things on a given day?

- Watching TV
- Reading a magazine
- Checking email
- Surfing the web
- Gossiping
- Shopping online
- Catching up on the news online

- Playing a game on the computer or smart phone
- Snacking
- Complaining about work, another person or life in general
- Staring off into space because you're so overwhelmed
- Looking up an old friend/enemy/boyfriend/girlfriend on Facebook

Yes? Then you have time to plan.

If taking time to plan is a new idea for you, once you've gotten through this entire book and have the tools you need, just commit to planning every work day for one week. Take ten minutes to plan and prioritize your tasks five days in a row. Once you've planned five days in a row, note whether your mental state was different on those days, and whether you got more of the right stuff done.

EXERCISE

Right now, put a brightly colored sticky note on this page. On the part of the note that sticks out of the book, write "Practice Planning." This is your reminder to come back and do this exercise when you have all the tools. You can skip this step if you already plan or feel like you can trust yourself to make planning a routine. This is for those who worry that this good idea will fall into the lake of good intentions instead of being something that actually improves your life.

Determining Your Destination

If where you'll go is the information you need when planning a vacation, how do you determine what your destination is in terms of your business?

For many, the destination in business terms is your "goal." I'm on board with that—sort of.

Goals are an important piece of information, but there's pre-work to do before you can start defining your goals.

In order for your goals to be worth striving for, they have to matter to you. In order for your goals to matter to you they have to be aligned with your core values.

You must know your core values and be in alignment with them if you want to be content with how you spend your time.

In this process to make you content with how you spend your time, we start with your core values and end up making meaningful decisions about how to spend your minutes. I call it the Making Minutes Matter Method™. In order for you to see how all of this fits together, here's an illustration:

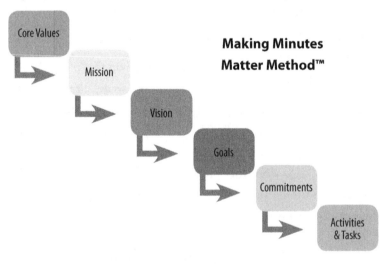

As we continue, we'll be talking in detail about each one of these steps.

First, there are two skills you must have in order to be successful in this busy world. They are Choosing and Focusing. We get into Choosing in Chapter Four.

Choosing

C hoosing is the first of the two skills you must have to experience the happiness that resides of the top half of the State of Mind Model. You're making dozens, even hundreds of choices a day and may not even realize it, though you may realize very intensely how exhausted you are. Making choices is tiring!

Not making choices just means you stand a significant chance of doing a lot of things that you don't like, don't value, or don't need to do.

How Do You Spend Your Minutes?

You have a say in how you spend your 1,440 minutes a day. So many of the choices made about time are focused on what will be done in the future. Whether the future is 15 minutes from now, tomorrow, next week or next year.

Every one of those 1,440 minutes is "now" at some point. In that now will you watch another TV show or go for a walk? Will you review your budget or surf the web? Will you worry about that weird sound your car is making or make an appointment to have it checked out? Will you stew over a disagreement or make a call to talk it out? Will you focus on how unkind life can be or do a kindness for someone else who is having a tough time? Will you shuffle stuff on your desk because you don't know what to do first or tackle just one thing—anything—on your task list?

In terms of action, "now" is all you get to make a difference in your life. Your past actions have an impact on where you are now, but they're still actions in the past. You can build on those actions—or apologize for them if it's something you regret—but you can't change them. And of course, you can always do things differently in the future, but again, what you *will* do matters much less than what you *are* doing.

The choices you make in this moment about what you do with your time, what you say, how you interact with people, etc., are what make the difference between success and failure, happiness and disappointment, progress and stalling.

How do you choose what you should be spending your minutes on? Sometimes it doesn't feel like a choice at all but something that's foisted upon you. Or time just goes by so fast that maybe choices were made but it didn't feel like it. Stuff just got done. Or didn't. Where did that time go?

Speed and overwhelm get in the way of using your minutes mindfully.

To be in control, and know that you're making thoughtful decisions about how you spend your minutes, you need clarity about things that impact you much more deeply than anything on a to-do list.

We're going to shift your decision-making platform from sand to bedrock. And it starts with your Core Values.

Core Values

There was a time when I just didn't get the whole Core Values thing. Perhaps because I didn't know enough about it. But more likely because I saw companies who said they had core values but weren't living them. That told me two things. First, that core values were only a marketing/branding exercise for businesses. And second, that in most cases the company had no intention of actually acting in accordance with those values.

It was a joke.

But right about the time I was crying at my kitchen counter about not having enough business, I was encouraged to go through an exercise to help me identify my own core values.

I did, and it's changed me forever.

Your core values guide all the decisions you make—and the choosing that you do—whether you know it or not. Being fully aware of those values makes decision-making and choosing how to spend your minutes clearer, easier, and most importantly, more rewarding.

Once I identified my core values, so many of my life decisions made sense. While those decisions felt right in my gut at the time, I often couldn't put my finger on why I made them.

In one job, (more than one, to be completely candid) I was doing work I found somewhat interesting that paid well and had nice benefits, but I quit because I found management intolerable. It wasn't a hard decision to make at the time, even though there were solid reasons to stick it out.

I discovered my core values when I read a short book by Tim Brownson called *Aligning with Your Core Values*. Since I read it, he's edited the book for use primarily by life coaches, but you can visit www.ADaringAdventure.com if you'd like to experience his process. I also guide business owners through the process if you want to collaborate on the effort. But you can get started right here.

In short, Core Values are guiding principles that dictate your behavior and can help you distinguish between right and wrong.

EXERCISE

Look at this list of sample core values and choose some that resonate with you. But before you do that, read just a little further to help guide your decisions.

Sample Core Values

Authenticity	Justice
Bravery	Kindness
Commitment	Knowledge
Community	Leadership
Connection	Love
Creativity	Nurturing
Diversity	Open-mindedness
Equality	Passion
Fairness	Patience
Family	Peace
Forgiveness	Persistence
Freedom	Positivity
Fun	Prudence
Gratitude	Self-control
Growth	Service
Happiness	Significance
Health	Security
Humor	Spirituality
Humility	Stability
Honesty	Trust
Integrity	Wisdom

This list is not exhaustive but is meant to help you get started. If you don't find enough words on here that resonate with you, an internet search can turn up dozens more. Just be careful not to overwhelm yourself with options. You may find that many, many of these matter to you. But some will seem to matter more than others. Take care not to choose words you think any good person should choose. Not choosing one of these core values doesn't mean you are against it, it just doesn't make it to the top of the list.

On your first pass circle as many as you like. Then do a second pass and winnow down the list until you're left with no more than eight. You may find that some of your first-pass choices are similar in meaning—which can help the winnowing process.

Remember, your core values are already in your gut so there's no need to overthink this. Your first instincts are powerful. You've subconsciously been making decisions based on these core values for a long time.

Once you have narrowed it down to eight, write them in the spaces of the chart on the following page in no particular order. If you prefer, you can download a copy or two (you'll do this exercise twice) of this chart at https://www.mckcoaching.com/mmm-resources/. Shortly, I'll walk you through a head-to-head comparison process.

	Value	Ranking							Totals
1		1	1	1	1	1	1	1	
		2	3	4	5	6	7	8	
2		2	2	2	2	2	2		___
		3	4	5	6	7	8		
3		3	3	3	3	3			___
		4	5	6	7	8			
4		4	4	4	4				___
		5	6	7	8				
5		5	5	5					___
		6	7	8					
6		6	6						___
		7	8						
7		7							___
		8							
8									___

When I first went through the process I narrowed the eight core values I had chosen down to my top three per Tim Brownson's instructions. I'll show you how to do that in the head-to-head comparison.

But because I *am* my business and my business must also be aligned with my core values, I expanded the number to seven. These additional values allow for all-encompassing guidelines for making decisions about how I can best serve, while being true to myself.

Here are my personal/professional core values:

Accountability—Delivering what I promise. Partnering with clients to hold them accountable as we work on what they want to achieve.

Authenticity—Showing who I am. Being open and transparent in conversations, negotiations and collaborations.

Growth—Growing myself, my business and being an active partner in the personal and professional growth my clients seek.

Merit—My actions must merit respect. My content must merit your attention. My work must merit my fee.

Simplicity—Unnecessary complexity hampers progress. Choose the simplest, most effective path for my business and my clients.

Kindness—Choosing to act with heart and empathy.

Humor—Business shouldn't be a slog. Put fun into business and lightness into life.

When I make decisions about my life and my business, I bump them up against my core values. If there's alignment, I move forward. If there isn't alignment, I take a step back and regroup.

When You're Not in Alignment

A few years ago, I began creating online training. I completed one course and hated every minute of the process. My plan was to create two more, but I kept putting off the work. I didn't even do what was necessary to promote the one I did complete.

I added online training to my service offerings as a method to help people who may not have the discretionary income to hire me as a trainer or coach. Additionally, in no small part, to make money while I slept. Seems reasonable to develop and sell that kind of a product, right?

But it felt very wrong.

Why?

Because it was so impersonal. It didn't feel authentic and I couldn't help buyers with accountability. I was doing it because many smart people said I should, not because I believed in its merit. It also added a level of complexity that drove me nuts. The process of creating it was anything but simple for me.

If I had sat quietly and considered online training and how it aligned with the core values of my business, I'd have saved myself a lot of time.

See how knowing what yours are could add so much insight into how you spend your time?

How Many Core Values Should You Have?

Back to you deciding how many core values are right for you. The short answer is no fewer than three and not more than eight.

You need a minimum of three to cover enough territory to guide your decision-making. For example, if "security" was your only core value, every decision you make would have to be tested against whether the outcome aligns with your ability to assure security. Not every decision will even impact security.

A maximum of eight is suggested because it's the upper end of feasibility when it comes to measuring adherence as you make choices.

You've selected eight and should you choose to stick with eight, you're good to go. If you want to narrow that list but are having a hard time ordering your list because they all matter to you, you can do the head-to-head comparison I mentioned earlier.

It's not a difficult exercise, but it's challenging to explain so I've created a short video that shows you how to do it.

You can find that video here. https://www.mckcoaching.com/mmm-resources/

Creating Short Definitions

It's helpful to create short definitions or descriptions of what each of your core values means to you.

By doing this, you can explain to yourself and perhaps to others how this value is manifested in your daily living.

In my view, the more concise you can be the better. Don't worry that you need to create pithy statements worthy of being engraved on gold plates. The days of corporate-speak are long over. Let you be you and write from your gut and your heart.

The definitions you write today are important, but you're not carving them into a tablet. If you decide to revise them later, you're the boss.

If you like, you can use the simple definitions I created for my core values as a guide. To drive home the point that these are not cast in stone, it's entirely possible that my definitions will have been altered on my website by the time this book is in print.

You Have Anti-Values, Too

There are also anti-values that guide you in very powerful ways. Anti-Values are those things that are simply intolerable to you. These are ways of thinking or behaving that are even more extreme than just rubbing you the wrong way.

Here is a list of anti-values to help you understand what I'm talking about:

Sample Anti-Values

Aggression	Hypocrisy
Anger	Ill health
Anxiety	Infidelity
Apathy	Immorality
Arrogance	Injustice
Betrayal	Intimidation
Brutality	Isolation
Conflict	Jealousy
Contempt	Laziness
Cruelty	Pain
Cynicism	Pomposity
Death	Poverty
Dishonesty	Procrastination
Disgust	Rudeness
Fear	Selfishness
Frivolity	Stress
Greed	Suspicion
Hate	Worry

Follow the same process as identifying your core values, but in this case, I recommend limiting yourself to three in the final form. Start by circling as many as you like. Then narrow it down to eight or less. If you need help getting to your top three, do the head-to-head comparison process again.

Here is a chart to use for your Anti-Values exercise:

	Value	Ranking							Totals
1		1	1	1	1	1	1	1	
		2	3	4	5	6	7	8	
2		2	2	2	2	2	2		___
		3	4	5	6	7	8		
3		3	3	3	3	3			___
		4	5	6	7	8			
4		4	4	4	4				___
		5	6	7	8				
5		5	5	5					___
		6	7	8					
6		6	6						___
		7	8						
7		7							___
		8							
8									___

Your three anti-values create intolerable visceral reactions in you when you align with them. This is just the opposite of your core values, which you want to be *in* alignment with. You want to be *out* of alignment with your anti-values.

My three anti-values are Betrayal, Selfishness, and Cruelty.

I cannot tolerate those behaviors in myself or in others. If, even unintentionally, I exhibit those behaviors, I must make it right in order to look myself in the mirror. If others exhibit those behaviors, I must ask for a change—and get it—or walk away from the person or business.

Here is an example of how a core value and anti-value worked together to help me understand a tough but inevitable decision.

I was on Facebook for years but always hated it. While there were some posts from friends and family that were fun to see, I often thought it was more of a 24/7 holiday newsletter. You know, the ones where the sender's job/children/vacation/life is always perfect.

But I stayed on it because I thought I should. For one, because it's a good platform for business marketing. And two, because not being on it would give the impression that I'm indifferent to what's going on with other people.

I vowed many, many times to get consistent with posting and reacting to other's posts. I broke the vow every single time.

Finally, the Cambridge Analytica scandal happened, and it made me mad. I downloaded the archive of information Facebook had on me and that was it. I wasn't even on Facebook very much and it had a ridiculous amount of information about me.

Though I realize other platforms also have tons of data about me, this was the excuse I needed to dump Facebook, and I did.

It was and is a gigantic load off my psyche. My core and anti-values shine a light on why that is.

Me pretending to enjoy Facebook and sometimes "liking" things because I thought I should, was me not being Authentic. Being on Facebook only because it might be good for my business was Selfish. I was out of alignment with a core value and in alignment with an anti-value. The relief at having this clarity is immeasurable.

EXERCISE

Look back at situations that had a powerful emotional impact in light of your core and/or anti values. What insights bubble to the surface? Take a few minutes to choose one or two incidents or choices and how your values were at play, even if you're only now realizing it.

Now, pat yourself on the back for doing the work to identify your core and anti-values. It's not easy! This is a perfect time for a moment of contentment. Revel in your accomplishment, even if only momentarily.

You've mixed the cement that helps to build your Mission. And that's what we cover next.

Mission

With clarity about your core and anti-values, next is creating your Mission.

Your mission statement is why you do what you do. It's the purpose of your business. What are you trying to achieve every day in the work you do? Why does your business exist?

If you're doing this exercise not as a business owner, but as an employee of a larger organization, you can still create a personal/professional mission statement. It's an eye-opening exercise because if your own mission statement is impossible to work toward in the organization where you currently work, perhaps a change is in order. Not in you, but in where you work.

Being aligned with your core values is everything. Your mission comes out of your core values. If your mission isn't in alignment with where you work or the work you do, you won't be in alignment with your core values, either. And tragically, you'll be forfeiting your opportunity for happiness and contentment at work.

Your mission statement may include some of your core value words, but it doesn't have to.

To give you a better idea, this is mine:

MCK Coaching + Training Mission

To teach the mindset, skills and processes to make every minute matter. To coach and train thoughtful communication skills to foster more meaningful and collaborative interactions.

EXERCISE

It's time for your crappy first draft. Start playing with this statement and don't worry that your first ones may be junk. I've written mine dozens, maybe over 100 times!

Vision

Your vision statement is what the world looks like when you accomplish your mission. When you look at the people around you, or your office, or your clients, and you have succeeded in your mission, what do you see?

Again, as an example, here is mine:

MCK Coaching + Training Vision

My clients and others I impact feel content with how they spend their time and are at ease and effective when interacting with others.

It's simple, yes?

It's all it needs to be. Remember, the definition of contentment is "a sense of peaceful happiness." When my clients and others I impact get that from any experience with my work, I can't ask for more. I have fulfilled my Mission.

EXERCISE

Your turn. When your Mission is achieved, what does your world like? Don't feel like you have to get the right sentences down right off the bat. Write as much as you like and edit later. It's much easier to edit than to create from scratch.

With your Core Values, Mission and Vision developed, you've established your bedrock foundation.

This is a big deal. Time for another moment of contentment!

Goals

Business and life are moving so fast that what's suffering is time to think about what you want to achieve in very specific terms.

But not for you, any longer!

What goes on top of a bedrock foundation? Structures. Buildings, houses, monuments, etc.

Now that you've gotten this far in the process, you'll have much more clarity to identify your "structures." These are your Goals.

Your goals are what you need to achieve to see your vision become a reality.

As I'm sure you've heard more than once, successful goals are SMART: Specific, Measurable, Achievable, Results-Focused and Timebound. Make the effort to break your goal(s) down into steps that fit those criteria, and you're ahead of the pack.

In my case, a basic Goal is how many coaching clients I want to serve in a year.

This is what that that looks like:

Specific: 10 coaching clients per month, minimum

Measurable: Can't get much easier than measuring an actual number. It's 10 or it's not. I either miss it, hit it, or exceed it.

Achievable: This is entirely do-able.

Results-Focused: Working with this number of clients results in me seeing my vision fulfilled for those clients.

Timebound: A month is a month. I can look at every month and see whether I met the goal or not.

How about a personal goal?

Perhaps you want to run a 10k.

Specific: I want to run/walk a 10k on *insert date here*

Measurable: Measure your progress along the way. Increase your distance a bit at a time knowing that by the race day you need to be able to cover the entire 10k.

Achievable: Even if you're a couch potato now, if you want to do this, you can. (If you don't want to do this, you should pick another goal.) Even if you had to walk some of it, a finish line is a finish line.

Results-Focused: All the training you do will be for the purpose of getting you prepared to finish that 10k.

Timebound: Race day is happening with or without you! You know exactly when you need to be ready to complete this goal.

To be sure, these are very simplistic goals. For both more detail is needed, but that's where your Commitments, Activities and Tasks come in, which we'll discuss later in this chapter.

You may be thinking, "How does running a 10k have anything to do with my mission and vision? Or my core values?" It doesn't directly. But feeling physically fit, strong, healthy, committed, accomplished—you choose your adjectives—can only help you as you strive for non-physical goals. Your body and mind are powerfully connected. Anything good you do for your body positively impacts your mind.

These are just two examples of goals. You likely have many more.

EXERCISE

First, write down some goals that you already know you have or ones that come to mind now that you've gotten clearer on your Mission and Vision.

Next, take one or two of those goals and make them SMART. You'll do that for all your goals, but for now practice with just a couple of them.

This process is like anything else you try for the first time or get back to after you haven't been doing it for a while. You need practice.

Play with these exercises some and don't make it too big and complicated. The more you set goals and break them down, the more comfortable you'll be with the process. Allow yourself baby steps if you need them.

Where Do You Go From Here?

Many well-intentioned people don't get as far as you've gotten already. Others get this far and chuck it all, reverting to old habits.

Not you! You've chosen what structures will be built on your bedrock.

What's next?

You must do the SMART steps and that takes Commitment. Goals are only achieved when you're *committed* to taking action. Attaching commitments to what you want to achieve is the next critical step to achieve your goals.

Commitments

Traditional advice is to start defining and completing tasks based on your goals. But, I contend there's an important step in between.

Create Commitments based on your goals. A commitment is a promise to yourself. It has teeth.

Commitment is active and strong. It says you have resolve.

Try it out loud. Pick a goal from the list you came up with and use it to fill in the blank below. First say,

"My goal is to _____."

As important as a goal is, it sounds a bit dreamy and aspirational.

Now try,

"I'm committed to _____."

That sounds concrete and action-oriented!

It's obviously important to have goals. I didn't ask you to create that list of goals to waste your valuable time. I just want you to try those statements out loud to make a point about how much words matter. Commitment is a word that says you're dedicated to making something happen.

Working with my coaching clients, Commitments are a critical part of the process. After each full coaching call, we mutually agree upon up to three commitments that they will focus on until our next full call two weeks later.

Those Commitments building upon one another week after week result in them experiencing the changes and accomplishments they seek.

Here are some examples of Commitments. You'll see that sometimes it's a physical task and other times it's a thinking or mindset task. They're both important!

- Pay attention to the urge to multitask. Reset and refocus.
- Practice not reacting immediately when triggered.
- Assemble list of responsibilities that could be delegated/offloaded.
- Run/walk minimum of two miles, three days a week.
- Assemble all random task lists and consolidate.
- Purposefully pause for 2 seconds after the other person stops talking to refrain from urge to interrupt.

A Commitment is an agreement you make with yourself to work on, focus on, or think about something that will help you advance toward your Goal.

Looking back at the Goal you chose and applied the SMART structure, what might be some things you need to commit to reach your Goal?

Remember my goal to serve a minimum of ten coaching clients a month? One of my commitments is to fully complete my weekly outreach sheet. That sheet lists the many activities I do to build and maintain business relationships. The Commitment is completing the sheet. The Tasks are what is listed on the sheet. I'll explain more about that shortly.

Goals and Commitments Must Work Together

A goal without commitment is a goal you probably won't reach. A commitment without a goal lacks direction. Like that destination-less vacation we talked about earlier. Without a goal, you have nothing concrete to which you are committed. Develop your goals and make commitments to get you closer and closer to reaching that goal.

To fulfill Commitments requires taking action. And that's where we go next.

Activities and Tasks

At the beginning of this chapter, we went over how you use your 1,440 minutes a day. On a literal level, you spend a good deal of those minutes on Activities and Tasks. Your never-ending To-do list, if you like.

Your Activities and Tasks are things you do to fulfill your Commitments in service of reaching your Goals—Goals which were created to see your Vision become a reality. That reality fulfills your Mission and allows you to live in alignment with your Core Values.

This chapter shared the process to help you get better at Choosing. Choosing is one of the two skills you must have in order to experience both accomplishment and contentment. I developed the Making Minutes Matter Method to help make choosing simpler and easier.

Armed with the work you've done defining everything from your values to your commitments, choose to do the activities and tasks required to meet your commitments and achieve those goals one step at a time. Narrow your focus, stay on track and do the *right* work.

Managing your Activities and Tasks is a process which I'll share with you in Chapter Six. Completing the right Activities and Tasks closes the loop that starts with you defining your Core Values.

Before you did all of this work, it may have seemed like a chasm to cross getting from that deeply personal Core Value space to checking things off of To-do list. But hopefully now it's not a chasm but a well-marked, purposefully-traveled path to your ideal destination.

A Word About Perfection

The need for perfection will stop you in your tracks, prevent any level of success, make you and people around you miserable.

Can you make a commitment right now to avoid striving for perfect?

You can strive for excellent, accurate, or superior, if you like. Just not perfect.

Here's why it matters.

Remember from Chapter Two: You can't be content if you're not doing your best. But neither will you be content if your best is never good enough.

Note that it says *your* best, not *the* best. Your best is as much as you can do. Your best may change from day-to-day depending on your physical state, workload, skill level, etc. *The* best is almost impossible to define in most cases. It's very often subjective. If you can't define it, you can't reach it.

As I wrote this book, my writing coach, Pam, supported my wish to call the first effort my Crappy First Draft. Calling it that took the pressure off me. I'd wanted to write a book for years, but thinking I needed to make it good from the first draft stopped me from writing anything at all.

In that case, I wasn't even trying for perfect—even wanting it to be good slammed the door shut on the process.

I was focused on creating *the* best draft, not *my* best draft. Sounds like I needed to read this section before it had even been written!

All or Nothing is Usually Nothing

There's a glitch in the thinking process that will destroy your best plans to follow through on your commitments.

The glitch is: Things have to be All or they don't count, and are therefore Nothing.

When you have a goal, the intention is to go for it 100%. Really commit yourself, right? So, when there's a small lapse or something is preventing you from forging ahead the way you planned, it seems easy to ditch that effort entirely and start again another time.

Do these statements sound familiar?

"I don't have time to make all the sales calls on my task list right now, so I'll do something else this morning and make all the calls this afternoon."

"I can't get a good workout in so, I'll just fit it in a full workout later."

"I don't have a big enough window of time to get my entire email inbox cleaned out now, so I'll do it when things are less busy."

"I ate a doughnut for breakfast so since the day is shot, I'll start again tomorrow. May as well eat whatever I want today and get it out of my system."

"My mind isn't in the right place to do a good job on this report, so I'll wait until I'm in a better frame of mind."

To beat that mindset, choose to think of what progress you can make with the time you have available. Incremental progress is progress!

Not only that, you don't have to wait until tomorrow to do things differently. Who says you must start every day in the morning? You can start your day over at any time of the day. You don't have to choose how to spend your minutes at just one specific time of day. Any minute is just as good as another to start over or re-set your mindset.

If you sometimes fall victim to the all or nothing mindset, slow down and actively think about the choices you're making and see if you can shift your thinking and your priorities so that you can have *incremental* success. You may end up giving 100%, just not all at one time.

Flexibility...to a Point

Being flexible is important. Though everyone benefits from planning on a macro (entire life) level and occasionally on a micro (by the minute) level—your most mindfully developed plans can change despite your best efforts. It's life. Being comfortable with a certain amount of flexibility is a good thing.

On the other hand, make certain you don't get so flexible that you lose your grip on what's genuinely important to you. You need to be aware of your non-negotiables.

Non-negotiables don't require flexibility because they are that important to you. You're solidly committed to responding to non-negotiables in a certain way.

If you don't identify your non-negotiables, little by little, day by day, you can let things slide and eventually lose sight entirely of what really matters to you.

I see it happen frequently.

Here are some examples of non-negotiables:

- Rick Steves, the travel expert, says "no" to any request for his time that falls outside of focus on his family or travel. He's asked to be on a softball team? Nope. Takes away time from family and travel.

- A successful business owner wouldn't work on Sundays. Ever. (He's since comfortably retired.) He knew once he started doing so he might get used to the revenue he could generate, or the jump start he could get on his Monday and it would be too hard to stop. For him, Sundays were for family and relaxing.

- A client who often brings work home says that if her young child asks for her time and she also has work to do, her child's request comes first. Putting him first sends a message to him that he's more important than her work when she's at home.

- One colleague only volunteers for one organization at a time. That way he can control his schedule and give full focus to the one organization.

- A client schedules sales call time on her calendar. It's a vitally important piece of her workload and she doesn't allow any other meeting requests or tasks to take over that block of time.

- A speaker gives one free speech per month. Twelve fee-waived speeches a year is a significant and generous commitment. Sought after and heavily booked, this speaker doesn't have to weigh opportunities and squeeze in additional freebies to be a nice guy while sacrificing revenue opportunities.

What those non-negotiables allow is an easy "no." So many decisions must be made every day. When you can eliminate some of them, do it.

EXERCISE

What are your non-negotiables? Take a few moments to think about those things that really matter to you. Perhaps you need to look back at your core values for some inspiration? You may only have one, or you might have several.

Choosing Means Yes. And No.

By definition, choosing one thing means you have other options that have not been chosen. Choosing is challenging because it can often feel like you're saying no to many things. It feels that way because you probably are.

Some things you choose not to do can be done by other people. Delegating is a wonderful thing. Here are ideal opportunities for delegating:

Tasks someone else can do more economically—Never refuse a task because it's "beneath" you. At the same time, consider what you earn in an hour—no matter whether you're hourly, salaried or work for yourself. As an example, if you make $225 an hour, is it an effective use of your time to gather lunch orders or mess with a printer issue? Time is better spent developing client solutions or making sales calls.

A lack of support does make it more difficult to delegate. But make sure you aren't doing tasks that aren't the best use of your time as a way to avoid complex or challenging tasks that can only be done by you.

Tasks that exhaust you—Handling the occasional task that wears you out can't be avoided. But if a regular task depletes your physical and mental energy every time, it's time to delegate. Hours are too precious to waste them catatonic from dealing with a task that sucks the life out of you.

Tasks someone else is more qualified to do—If you're a business owner and your business is anything other than building websites, you'd be wise to hire a professional to build your website.

The professional with website expertise will get it done it in a fraction of the time and result in a higher quality product.

- When you consider what you may be able to delegate, ask yourself these questions:
- What can someone else take over from me right now?
- What can someone else take over with a bit of training?
- What responsibilities do I have that someone else might find rewarding to take on?
- What can *only* I do?

Everyone in an organization has roles and responsibilities—even if you are an organization of one. Assign tasks in alignment with skills and bottom line impact. Delegate or hire people to take on what you shouldn't be doing.

Maybe No One Should Be Doing It

"We've just always done it," is a statement that begs deeper consideration. Nothing should be done simply because it's been done for a long while. Is the task necessary? If you don't see the need for it, does anyone else? Review routines occasionally and look for opportunities to streamline.

Just Say No

Getting comfortable saying no pays off in found time. When you say no to things you don't want to do, you get back some of your 1,440 daily minutes.

You may find it hard to say no because you want to be a team player or be seen as helpful or just want to be liked. If someone stops liking you because you say no, that was a pretty fragile relationship, don't you think?

Pick situations when you truly have a choice (it's more often than you may think) and practice saying. "Thanks for thinking of me, but no, that's not something I can do right now."

Then stop talking. No need to explain your reasons. No is no. A kind but firm no is all you need.

If you want to do something, but not want they asked, you can add, but "here's what I *can* do."

EXERCISE

First, just practice saying no. To feel better about it, note your body language. You don't have to say no with a stern look on your face and your arms crossed across your chest. Practice saying the words along with body language that still conveys kindness and it will be more comfortable,

The other thing you're practicing is to stop talking after you make the statement. It's tempting to explain yourself, but you don't need to.

Once you've practiced and feel more comfortable, try it in a real situation. When, based on all the work you've done thus far in this book, you recognize a situation where no is appropriate, say so.

When you do, come back here and make some notes about how it went. How did you feel when you said it? How did you feel after? Did the work still get done or role get filled? How is your relationship with the person who asked you?

Many times, the trepidation you had wasn't even warranted. Saying no ends up working out just fine.

Quitting

You know what they say…

"Winners never quit, and quitters never win."

That's stupid.

Smart people know when to quit and aren't hesitant or embarrassed to do so. Don't let people guilt you into continuing with something that you know isn't right for you. Don't force yourself to keep plugging away at something because you paid good money or there's no one to replace you or you're afraid to disappoint people.

Quitting takes courage. It takes courage to say,

"This isn't working for me any longer, so I need to step back."

"This job/project/idea/commitment has become unworkable."

"The debate is never going to result in mutual understanding, so I'm going to let it go."

"I thought I wanted this but now that I'm actually pursuing it, I don't want it after all.

As a quitter you do win because once you stop doing or pursuing something that no longer serves you, you have time to spend on things that DO serve you. Trade commitments that drain you for commitments that energize you. Maybe calling it "trading" rather than quitting makes it more comfortable to own, but quitting is okay.

I quit things frequently in my business, and so far those choices have been nothing but a relief.

Don't be afraid to be a quitter.

Feeling as Though You Have No Choice

Many years ago, my very young son was in speech therapy. We adopted him from Russia and he had no speech or language skills. We were working to get him up to speed before kindergarten started.

Another mom also had a child in the speech therapy session. She had three young children to my one. So, during the speech therapy class she was often entertaining or corralling her other two kids.

One day she came rushing into the building, clearly stressed. She was running late and had far too many things to handle at one time. She was overwhelmed and feeling defeated. Most moms and dads can relate to that feeling.

She said at one point. "This is too much, but I just don't have a choice."

Which started us talking about choice. The reality is she did have a choice. Some parents wouldn't bother with speech therapy and instead let the kid sit in front of a TV. Other parents might bring the child to speech therapy, and spend the time screaming at the other two simply because of overwhelm.

It wasn't that she didn't have a choice. She was just making the responsible, selfless choice. A choice that, for that day, made her feel exhausted.

When she looked at it that way, she felt differently. No less tired, but no longer a victim, either.

When you're feeling like you have no choice, think again. Do you really have no choice, or is it just that the right choice for you isn't the easy way out?

Being proactively involved in making choices about how you spend your time gives the power back to you, where it belongs.

What we've gone over so far boils down to choosing how you spend your minutes. We've established the need for goals. To reach those goals, you develop commitments that point you in that direction. The activities and tasks you do every day allow you to meet your commitments and achieve your goals. Pretty simple, right?

But there's another challenge that stands in the way.

The ability to Choose is one of two skills you need to have to be successful in this fast-paced, information-intensive world.

The second skill?

Focus.

CHAPTER FIVE

Focusing

Focus is important. In fact, in some jobs the ability to focus on the right thing at the right time can mean the difference between life and death.

The Sterile Cockpit

Take pilots for instance. Landing an aircraft with hundreds of passengers is a good time to be thinking about nothing but getting the plane safely down on the correct runway, across the tarmac without incident and to the assigned gate.

That's why in 1981 the FAA established the "Sterile Cockpit Rule". This regulation prohibits crew members from performing "non-essential duties or activities while the aircraft is involved in taxi, takeoff, landing, and all other flight operations conducted below 10,000 feet, except cruise flight."

Since the initiation of this regulation, studies have been done to determine whether non-adherence to the rule has been at the root of aviation incidents both significant and minor. It bears mentioning that non-adherence to the Sterile Cockpit Rule is usually not intentional. Four general categories of distraction are mentioned as reasons the rule is violated:

1. A casual conversation started above 10,000 feet continues into descent

2. A flight attendant unexpectedly visits the cockpit or calls on the interphone

3. Non-essential radio calls and PA announcements

4. Sight-seeing

So why does this matter to you if you're not a pilot or passenger?

Because your job is important too, even if you aren't making life and death judgment calls. You're faced with distractions all day, every day. And those distractions can exact a heavy cost.

Distractions are Constant

You sit down at your desk in the morning and have every intention of working on the most important task on your to-do list. But before you get started you decide to make a quick check into email or maybe your social media feed or a news website. Something you see while doing this rooting around inspires you to look into something else. And you're off. The next conscious thought will be "Where on earth did the morning go?"

It happens to all but the most disciplined people.

This chapter about Focus looks at two things:

1. What kinds of things infringe on your ability to Focus;

2. Strategies to get your Focus back.

Think about how often you experience these focus-killers:

Smartphone—According to Deloitte, the average person checks his/her phone 46 times per day. Assuming you sleep for six hours a night that averages out to checking your phone 2.5 times an hour. That's a lot of interruptions. Most people are looking at the phone out of habit, not necessity. How about you?

Computer—Whether it dings every time you get an email or just sits there tempting you, there's no end to the distractions a computer offers. Email to read or clean out, files to re-organize, web searches to be done. Is your computer both a necessary business tool and a frustrating source of distraction?

People—Stopping by your office to chat, instant messaging, calling every half hour to get an answer they need to keep their project moving forward. Interruptions are constant which makes being able to focus, confounding.

Overwhelm—Too many tasks, too many projects, too many commitments, too many deadlines, too many ideas. Too many things vying for your attention. You can't focus if there is too much in the file cabinet that is your brain.

Disorganization—Physical disorganization creates mental disorganization. If your office or desk is out of control, it's likely to impact your ability to focus. I've even worked with people where the disorganization was at home and it still affected their focus at work. Clutter and disarray, though physical, do affect your mental state, too.

Lack of Systems and Processes—Not having systems and processes to rely on requires your brain to work too hard on repetitive things, leaving you less brain power for original, solution-oriented thinking.

You—Being tired, angry, sad, hungry, thirsty, too full, overly caffeinated or hepped-up on sugar make a dramatic difference in your ability to focus.

In the chapters to come, I'll share ideas for overcoming most of these challenges. Because physical clutter can be a big enough challenge that entire books are written on that subject alone, I won't go into that one. If that's your challenge, pick up a book that shows you how to get your stuff under control or perhaps even hire a professional organizer.

Preparing to Focus vs. Procrastination

Chapter Seven is entirely about overcoming procrastination. But while we're talking about focus, there's one procrastination-oriented topic to discuss here.

Recognizing the difference between preparation and procrastination.

You may sometimes identify activities you're doing as preparing you to be better able to focus. Sometimes they are. But you must recognize the difference, or you can spend hours "preparing" when what you're really doing is "avoiding."

Does This Sound Familiar?

You've got a deadline looming for a challenging project. You know that the ability to do a good job will be compromised if you don't give yourself ample time, so you commit to start today.

You want to have a clear head to do the work, so you tackle one or more things first so you can properly focus.

It feels reasonable, but are these tasks part of your preparation? Or are they better defined as procrastination?

Here's a list of tasks that qualify as procrastination:

- Cleaning out your desk drawer(s)
- Researching a conference you just learned about
- Refilling supplies
- Making folder labels
- Organizing paper clips
- Searching for your favorite pen
- Making or returning non-urgent calls
- Having a snack—unless your stomach is growling, or you feel faint

- Surfing the web for "more project data"
- Picking out good "focus" background music
- If you work out of your home—any type of household chore

These activities more often qualify as preparation:
- Cleaning off your desk—quickly, though
- Assembling and organizing project materials
- Creating a mindmap or other type of project plan
- Noting dates on your calendar for specific interim deadlines associated with the project
- Reviewing last year's final product and/or current materials

Cleaning off your desk can fall into both categories. If you take it too far it can be procrastination. But having a clear surface on which to work allows for your brain to feel clear as well. It also prevents having other things in your field of vision that you need to get done, which can distract you from the work at hand.

You must be honest with yourself, as I had to be when writing this book. It sometimes felt so daunting that I had to stop myself from spending writing time on anything *but* writing.

While files do need to be cleaned out and that's legitimate work to be done *at some time,* it's impossible to make the argument that doing so would ever take precedence over getting a deadline-driven project started or finished.

Let's go back to that list of focus-killers and tackle them.

Internal Interruptions

Internal interruptions are distractions that you cause yourself. External interruptions come from other people. We'll talk more about external interruptions in a minute, but right now here's a scenario describing a common internal interruption.

You've planned your day and selected your top priority task. You're ready to jump in and work on it. But the task is something you're not terribly fond of doing. Maybe it's going to take a lot of mental energy or it's just not your favorite type of work. So, you decide to check email quickly just to make certain something more important hasn't come in that would take precedence over what you're about to start doing.

And there it is.

You're not checking email because you need to—you're checking email because it's a "legitimate" way of putting off doing more important but unpleasant tasks. You know how I know this? Because I've done it, too. Everybody does!

E-mail can be intrusive, but just as often you manufacture the intrusion as a distraction.

Pay attention and make adjustments if you see yourself falling into that trap. In this case, awareness—and calling yourself out on it—is the first step to stopping.

And for heaven's sake, turn off any and all audible notifications that you've received new emails. The sound turns you into Pavlov's Dog and the pull to look at what just came in is overwhelming.

The likelihood is slim that any new email is critical enough to merit distracting you from your plan of action.

Computer and Web Distractions

Keeping too many windows open at one time just invites you to bounce around. Minimize what you don't need. It's the electronic version of cleaning off your desk.

StayFocusd is a Google chrome extension preventing you from surfing the web for a period of time that you set in advance. If you try to access a website when StayFocusd is enabled, you'll get a message reading "Shouldn't you be working?"

It takes just seconds to install and doesn't cost a penny—though you can make a donation if you like.

Not a Chrome user? You can find other options here. https://www.mckcoaching.com/mmm-resources/

Any one of those is an invisible helper to prevent web distractions.

Cueing Devices

In many cases, you don't even realize you've lost your focus. You're busy getting things done and that feels pretty good.

It becomes painfully clear later, when you reflect on your outcomes—what you intended to do is not what you actually did.

Maintaining your focus is a skill, and any skill can get better and feel more natural. But getting better requires practice and you must *remember* to practice.

Have you ever committed to drinking eight glasses of water a day and failed to do it? You failed not because you *refused* to drink the water but because you didn't *remember* to drink the water.

There's a big difference between refusing to focus and forgetting to focus. To help you remember to focus, you need a cueing device.

A cueing device is simply something to remind you to do what you are committed to doing.

I stack rubber bands around the top half of my water bottle. Every time I drain the bottle I move a rubber band to the bottom half of the bottle. By the end of the day all of the rubber bands should be moved from top to bottom. The rubber bands are my cueing device.

Choose a cueing device to help you remember to focus.

It can be as simple as a sticky note with the word "FOCUS" on it. You can choose a knick-knack on your desk to be your reminder to focus. Or you can print and display this sign. Here's a link to resources page where you'll find a pdf if you'd like to download a copy: https://www.mckcoaching.com/mmm-resources/

Every time you happen to glance at your cueing device, ask yourself, "Is what I'm doing right now where I need to be focusing my time and energy in this moment?"

If it is, great. If you find you've gotten yourself distracted, reset and refocus.

Training yourself to focus will take some time. It's a perfect Commitment to set for yourself.

EXERCISE

Choose your cueing device and commit to practicing your ability to focus for one week. Don't pile on anything else to practice that week. Just focus on focusing. When that week is up, commit to practicing for another week.

You'll experience more success by recommitting every week for a month than you will if you just say you'll practice for a month. It's a subtle but powerful difference.

External Interruptions

You are, essentially, your internal interrupter. Stealing your own focus. The biggest external decimator of your focus?

People.

I've never been in an office environment where people aren't frustrated by the number of interruptions they experience in a day. Studies show that when you are interrupted it takes and average of 23 minutes and 15 seconds to get back on task.

No wonder it's frustrating.

Here are two methods to take back control of your time:

The Preemptive Strike

Often a conversation starts and goes in a direction that makes it difficult to cut it off. For instance, a friend at work starts to talk about something that's upsetting her. Could be a co-worker, or maybe something going on at home. You want to be supportive, so you welcome her in to talk. But fifteen minutes later you're starting to feel anxious because you really need to get back to your work. But because she's mid-story, it feels rude to cut her off.

The Preemptive Strike sets you up to make shifting the conversation more comfortable.

When someone wants to talk with you, ask "How much time do you need?" Let's just say she says, "About ten minutes." Now you can decide if you have ten minutes or not. If you're under the gun and don't, suggest that you get together when you'll be better able to focus on the conversation.

If you feel like you do have ten minutes, she can feel free to share what's on her mind. From here there are two possibilities. 1) When ten minutes are up, the conversation is complete and you both get back to work. 2) She underestimated the time she needed and is continuing to talk beyond that ten-minute limit.

Number two could be awkward without the Preemptive Strike. But now, because you've laid the groundwork that you have only ten minutes, it's infinitely more comfortable to interrupt with, "Looks like we might need more than ten minutes. I really have to get back to this project, so let's set up a time to continue this conversation later. I want to be able to give you my full focus."

What might also happen is that as soon as you ask how much time she needs, she'll decide that now isn't the best time if it isn't a truly urgent conversation she needs to have.

The idea behind the Preemptive Strike is twofold. First, to control your time from the start. Know how much time you can spare and share that information with the other person. And two, I call myself a coach and confidant because people in the workplace sometimes need someone to confide things to. Having a friend at work that you can turn to when you need to vent is a tremendously comforting thing. Sensitive issues are going to come up and you'd do well not to fight that. The Preemptive Strike just allows for the conversations to happen in the right time.

If everyone in your office, department, work group, or company employs this strategy, it will get easier and easier to use. It never feels like an interruption when *you* need to talk. But it often feels like an interruption when *someone else* needs to talk. This strategy helps co-workers recognize that one person's need to talk could be viewed as an interruption instead of a welcome conversation.

Focus Time

Everyone needs quiet time to focus. When you're interrupted during time you had planned to get your head into a project, it's frustrating. But when you need an answer in order to keep moving forward, interrupting others happens almost without thinking. "I just need a minute." Or "Just need a quick answer to this question."

But like I said earlier, that quick interruption is going to exact a much bigger loss of time.

Create an office environment where everyone has focus time and everyone respects that need.

Many years ago, a guy invented what he called Protoblocs. (Sadly, they no longer exist.) It was a set of "blocks" distributed to each employee. The stack included a red cube, a yellow sphere and a green pyramid. On the corner of your desk nearest the door you placed the block that indicated your level of availability.

Green pyramid: Come on in.

Yellow sphere: I'd prefer not to be interrupted, but if it's important come in.

Red cube: Don't disturb me unless you're bleeding or the building is on fire.

Without speaking a word, colleagues would understand and respect one another's need for focus time.

You don't need to have blocks to do this. Any universally understood system for an office works. It helps everyone see that everyone needs focus time and that Bob's focus time needs to be honored even if it isn't the same as your focus time.

A Focus Time sign can be distributed to everyone in the office. Here's a link to a resource page where you can download and print a sign for your office:

https://www.mckcoaching.com/mmm-resources/

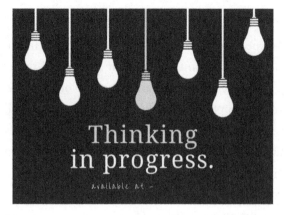

With this sign, you can post it outside your door or on your cube and add a sticky note letting co-workers know when you'll be available again.

Blocking Your Calendar

If co-workers have access to one another's calendars, that's also a great option for blocking out focus time. Everyone has to get in the habit of checking calendars before dropping in, but it can be done. Once you start to see how productive you can be when you're interrupted less, you'll be invested in returning the favor.

You Can Do Anything for 15 Minutes!

That was the maddening but effective response from my friend and trainer, Val, when she'd hear us complain about doing just a few more burpees or running one more hill in her brutal but effective boot camp. She was always right.

Focusing for long periods of time can be daunting. But you can definitely focus for 15 minutes.

For example, need to get started on a proposal or report? Set a timer for 15 minutes and focus like a laser-beam until you hear the "ding." Let the phone go to voice mail, shut your door, ignore your wristwatch and FOCUS. When you hear the bell, move on to something else if you wish.

Is your financial paperwork way behind? Same process. Set the timer and focus. You choose the amount of time you can allot for this laser-like focus time.

I strongly recommend an actual kitchen timer for this method. You can set it and forget it until it dings. Yes, I know you have a timer on your phone, but as crazy as this may sound, in the time it takes for you to pick up your phone and navigate to the timer app, it's highly likely you'll get distracted by email or news.

True story: I respond particularly well to a kitchen timer due to a "game" my mom used to play when I was a kid. I have four older siblings and we all had chores assigned to us. Like any kids, we tried to put off doing the chores as long as possible. My mom, who had a tremendous sense of humor, used a kitchen timer to motivate us. She called the game we played "Beat the Clock or Beat the Kid." Of course, none of us every got beaten, but not being entirely certain we wouldn't, we did our chores!

Pomodoro Technique

Though I've been using this method most of my life as well as coaching and training clients to do the same, it turns out there's a name for this idea: The Pomodoro Technique. Developed by Francesco Cirillo in the 1980s, it's called Pomodoro because the kitchen timer he used looked like a tomato. "Pomodoro" is "tomato" in Italian, and I suppose that sounds a lot cooler than The Tomato Technique.

His suggestion is to break up work into 25-minute segments—or Pomodoros—which cannot be interrupted—nor can they be stretched. I'm not as strict on a segment being exactly 25 minutes.

It's important to choose an amount of time that allows you to get things done without jeopardizing your ability to stay focused. Maybe you can focus for two hours and you need that time to be able to make significant progress. Set your timer for two hours. You make the rules here.

Recovery Breaks

When your timer dings, take a 2 or 3-minute break to refresh your body and brain. Get up from your chair, grab a drink of water, top off your coffee, stretch, etc. Letting your brain have a break is as important as your focus time. Even if you aren't using laser focus time, breaks are important. You'll come back sharper and clearer if you let your brain have recovery breaks.

EXERCISE

Choose something you need to get going on and try this technique. First, get yourself a kitchen timer. Next, choose a task or project that would benefit from you giving it your undivided attention. Set the timer and go.

Once you've tried this a time or two, take a few minutes to reflect on your experience doing it. Did the timer help? Did you find yourself losing focus and need to recommit yourself during the period you'd set aside? Did you accomplish more than you thought you would? Less?

Teaming Up

One summer my high school aged son and I tackled some projects around the house in between my work commitments. The result of one of our projects?—A porch-full of items for charity. I wanted to get rid of that stuff for a long while. But working with him was the spark that made it happen.

Another time, while working with a client, we tackled an office project that had been weighing on his mind. As we worked on it, he looked at me and asked, "Why is this so much easier when you're here?"

In both cases the reason we had so much success is because there were two of us.

When you have someone to back you up on a project, many of the roadblocks disappear. With a project partner you have someone to bounce ideas off of, keep you focused, take momentary breaks with you to restore your energy, think of strategies you may not have come up with on your own, and to hold you accountable for your choices.

If you've been putting off a project and it's eating away at you, get some help. Create a temporary partnership to make the going easier and to keep you focused. What you'll likely find is that whomever you ask for help will be happy to do so and may even ask you to return the favor.

The following are ideas about making the most of an accountability partner.

Accountability Partners—Temporary

Urgent tasks are easier to focus on. The deadline itself motivates you to stay on task and get things done. But what about tasks that are very important but not urgent? They're important so they must get done, but they have no actual deadline, so they get delayed over and over again.

Here's how you can make progress on that type of work:

1. Set a clear, defined deadline. Create a deadline as if getting this thing done really matters, because it does. It's the important but not urgent work that *builds* a business. Make the

deadline ambitious. To light a fire under yourself time has to be limited.

2. If no one else is expecting to see this work, which is usually the case, involve someone else in your commitment anyway. Someone you'd prefer not think of you as a slacking procrastinator. It's fine to tell the person what you're doing. "I've been putting off this task but now I'm committing to get it done and I'll follow up with you to let you know it's complete."

A colleague and I used to dread developing proposals, so we'd serve in this capacity for each other. I did—and do—have a great deal of respect for him. When I said I was going to do something, I was motivated to follow-through if only to save face.

Since then, I changed my business model, so I rarely have to write proposals and when I do, they're a single page. But not everyone can change the business model to suit their own needs. If you can't, and therefore have to do tasks that you'd prefer to put off, make use of an accountability partner.

Accountability Partners—Long Term

In the 19 years I've had my own business, I've had several long-term accountability partners. Some have been successful partnerships and others not. Right now, I'm in a great one. From the trenches, these tips will improve your chance of success:

1. **Limit it to two people.** There are several reasons for this, which you'll see in #2 and #4, but first it's because you can't back out of your accountability meeting as easily. I run with a bunch of friends and if there are more than two of us meeting for a run it's much easier for one person to bail. The thought being, "Well, even if I don't show up, there will still be other

people there to run with, so bagging it is no big deal." But if there are just two of us running, bailing means the other person is left running alone. Uncool. If there are only two in your accountability partnership you HAVE to show up.

2. **Agree upon a consistent day, time, duration and method of meeting.** My accountability partner and I have a phone call on Mondays at 9:00 am CST for 30 minutes. We alternate who initiates the call every six months. Going back to the "only two people" idea, it's much easier to agree on a day and time that works when you're only looking at two calendars.

3. **Put the meeting on your calendar and treat it like a client appointment.** We rarely shift our meeting day and time. This is a commitment and we treat it that way. I book clients around our accountability meeting. If you can't commit to a consistent meeting day, maybe you're just not committed enough to the partnership and this just isn't for you.

4. **Decide how flexible you'll be regarding the duration of your call.** Ours is booked for 30 minutes but we can alert the other person that "today it needs to be an 8-minute call" if needed. No hard feelings if we don't have time for a lengthy conversation. That flexibility makes it even easier to commit to the call no matter what else comes up. Only having two of us means we can be very efficient when we need to be.

5. **Decide what your commitments will look like.** I decided early on that I would list no more than three commitments each week and they have to be tasks I need to be held accountable for. Nobody needs to be held accountable to check email. My accountability partner decided that three items work for him, too. The focus on just a few critical tasks

is, well, critical. Commit to too much and you'll fail every week. Be realistic.

6. **Think about how you'll update one another about your progress on your commitments.** Sometimes we email each other on Friday afternoons and sometimes we update each other on the call on Monday. That part is flexible, and it works for us.

7. **Decide how you want the other person to deal with you** if you don't do the things you said you were going to do. Some people want no feedback at all. (I don't get that, but it works for them.) If I don't do what I said I was going to do, I want to be questioned about why. It's uncomfortable to make lame excuses, and the threat of looking bad to my accountability partner keeps me motivated. Do the work and I don't have to feel uncomfortable. That simple. Your partner may want to be handled differently. Just know what you both need.

8. **Don't get *too* close.** I consider my accountability partner a friend but not so close a friend that he makes excuses for me. "Oh, you've been going through a lot so it's okay that you haven't done what you said you were going to do for the last month." That's what wine with friends is for. Accountability partners are to keep you accountable.

9. **Occasionally review the partnership** and decide what's working and what may need to be adjusted. Work and life situations evolve, and your partnership will evolve, too. We regrouped when we saw our follow-through slipping a bit. Catch that early and make the necessary tweaks.

EXERCISE

Do you need a temporary or long-term accountability partner? Who else do you know who might be interested in that arrangement? Before you reach out to someone, think about how you would use and benefit from that collaboration. Go into to the conversation with your potential accountability partner with some thoughts about how it could work so you have a starting point. Negotiation and compromise are good. Make certain that whatever you set up fills the needs you both have. If you're looking for a partnership that focuses entirely on your needs and keeping you accountable, consider a business coach. I know one who would love to help you.

Employ the ideas in this Chapter and improve your ability to Focus. Focusing takes brain power, so you want to use that power as efficiently as possible. You can conserve brain power by having simple, effective processes and established routines to follow. That's what we're talking about in Chapter Six.

Routines and Processes

Everything you've created so far has been working toward you being able to create a plan for how you spend your minutes. Sometimes you'll want to make certain you're using those minutes as efficiently as possible.

Notice I say sometimes. I don't believe that being super-efficient all the time is necessary unless that's what makes you happy. I don't much care if my leisure time is spent efficiently. But having more leisure time is nice, which can happen if work is done more efficiently.

Routines and Processes help you get more of the right things done in less time and with less turmoil and stress.

Let's talk about the difference between Routines and Processes.

A routine is a typical order in which you do things.

A process is a step-by-step plan to accomplish a specific job.

It may help to think of a process as a more detailed and specific sub-step of a routine.

For instance, your routine may be to review website analytics and social media statistics on the 20th of every month. The specific data you're looking for in those analytics and statistics would be a part of your process. The process might include looking at last month's data, reviewing annual trends, comparing spikes to content, etc.

Or your routine may be to assess your KPIs (Key Performance Indicators) quarterly. The reports you run and the specific data you review would be part of a step-by-step process.

Routines and processes take even minor guesswork out of what you do when, and how you do it.

But That's So Predictable and Boring

"I have to be spontaneous. Structure saps my creativity. Routine is boring."

I hear this frequently from creative people, but the thinking is flawed. You boost creativity by utilizing structure. Established routines and processes serve two important functions:

1. Doing specific things at certain times of the day, following processes, even adhering to checklists means you think less about when and how to do those activities. You save brain power that you can now use on the interesting, creative side of business.

2. Because you're following a process, the routine perhaps boring things are accomplished more efficiently, which frees up time for more creative tasks.

Successful creative people follow routines and adhere to processes. A famous quote—attributed to many writers with no definitive ownership—says it perfectly: *I write only when inspiration strikes. Fortunately, it strikes every morning at nine o'clock sharp.*

Habits vs Routines

Before we go deeper into Routines and Processes, let's talk for a minute about Habits. There's a lot of buzz about creating better habits, and tons of books on how to do it better. But I'm not on board with the whole "habit" idea, as I stated earlier.

By definition, calling something a habit means that you do it without thinking about it. It's just automatic. Habits include putting on your seat belt, driving the regular route to and from work, placing your napkin in your lap, and lighting a cigarette—not a good habit, but then not all habits are.

When you try to create habits, you run into trouble. Because it's a "habit" you expect that you'll do this thing automatically, without having to consciously walk yourself through the steps to completion. Think about how much you've heard about developing better habits for eating, exercise, handling email, and managing your to-do list. Those activities aren't as simple as putting on your seat belt.

I provided insight into the "21 Days to a New Habit Myth" in Chapter One. If you need a refresher, hop back there and read that section.

If you've been expecting that you'll create and stick to a new habit in 21 days, you've been holding yourself to a standard that doesn't even exist!

You can create or change habits, but it's difficult – and a lot of work. Very few things must be habits in order to get the results you want. Save your energy. What you need is a solid, predictable routine, not a new habit.

If you want to eat more healthy foods then you create routines around meal planning, grocery shopping, and preparing meals. If you want to get in better shape you create routines around when you'll pack your gym bag, what days and times you'll hit the gym or go for a run. If you want to get to work on time, you create a morning routine for all the things you need to do to get out the door.

I call these Routine Reminders.

Routine Reminders

What can you turn into a routine to free up your brain for tasks that will truly benefit from a more creative approach?

- Morning routine (before you head out the door to work)
- Bedtime routine
- Weekly errands (gas, grocery, dry cleaning, etc.)
- Financial Status Review
- Marketing Review
- Sales Report Review
- Mid-year and End-of-year Review
- Monthly meetings
- Social media posting

EXERCISE

Either choose something you think of yourself or select one of the items above that would benefit from a Routine Reminder. List the steps that you will routinely follow. Don't worry about it being perfectly comprehensive on your first draft. As you go through the routine you may find additional steps to add. For a time, it's a work in progress.

Quick Start and Wrap Up Routines

How much more contentment would you experience if your workday started and ended focused and organized?

Right now, it may be more like this:

Walk into office. Check email. Get caught up on email for an hour. Realize that you have your first meeting in five minutes. Frantically search your desk for your notes – your mind not fully engaged in the search because you're concerned about being late.

Rush off to the meeting with part or none of your notes—thoughts scattered trying to get your head in the right frame of mind.

Obviously, there's a better way to start the morning and it's pretty simple.

Create routine checklists that allow you to go on autopilot at the start and end of your workday. Quick Start and Wrap Up Routines give you a repeatable process to be as focused and efficient as possible both when you get to your desk, and right before you leave it.

Take packing for a camping trip. How much easier would it be to have a list of things you need to do to get ready? Buying supplies, checking gear, packing the car, making campsite reservations, etc. You know to do all of it without a list, but the list makes it so much easier. Limit what taxes your brain. If you can create a routine and make a list to remind you of that routine, you're saving brainpower.

The items on the sample lists below may seem somewhat obvious, but having them written down on a small cheat sheet in front of you helps you glide into and out of the day,

Here's a sample of a Quick Start Routine:

- Empty briefcase/tote
- Review calendar for the day
- Select most important tasks to complete throughout the day
- Check and respond to voice mails
- Quick check of email looking only for high priority items
- Fill up water bottle (fatigue is one of the first signs of dehydration)

Your Wrap Up Routine may look something like this:

- Declutter desk and re-file papers and folders
- Gather papers/files to take home if necessary (hopefully not, so you can spend time relaxing and be refreshed the next day)
- Review appointments and your task list from the day and note follow-up items on to-do list
- Check email
- Check calendar for early appointments the next day and pull files/information, put on desk

A Wrap Up Routine allows you to make a clean break from the workday. It clears your mind and sets you up to have a more relaxed evening, knowing you closed up shop up efficiently and didn't miss important details.

EXERCISE

If your day would benefit from having these simple Routines, create them for yourself. Print them out on small piece of paper and post it where you can easily glance at them. Having the Quick Start and Wrap Up checklists out where you can see them will help you remember to do this new routine. Over time, you may need to look at the lists less frequently. But you'll also be glad you have them if for any reason your routine gets botched up due to a period of crazy busy-ness. They serve as reminders to get back on the track that was working for you.

Processes

Recurring activities that don't require creativity are best done following a process. Processes should include all the clearly defined steps you take in a particular order to get the job done. Your routine would include a consistent time and/or day of the month that you do the process. Think of monthly bank reconciliations or payroll processing as examples. You do those things on a certain day of the month and you follow a defined process to complete the work. The following activities are ideal to turn into repeatable processes:

- Preparation for a recurring meeting
- Networking follow-up
- Handling e-mail
- Monthly accounting tasks
- Interacting on social media
- Sales process
- Client intake
- Employee on-boarding
- Generating financial reports

I use many processes in my business. One of the most vital is my client onboarding process. It's not difficult to onboard a client, but there are a lot of steps on my end. I've created a comprehensive process that covers every step I need to take to make certain all bases are covered. I simply pull out the process and mentally check off each item as I complete it.

When you find yourself doing the same activity over and over, think about how you can turn it into a process. You'll get those activities completed faster, and safeguard against forgetting a step.

EXERCISE

Choose one of your activities that's regularly repeated and create a process you can follow. Include anything that you might have to look up as you go through the process. For instance, one of my steps includes sharing links with my new client, so the links are included as part of the process. I don't have to hunt them down.

Managing Tasks on a To-Do List

The worst to-do lists are on miscellaneous scraps of paper and no-longer-sticky sticky notes littering your desk. Or several lists on various pages of multiple legal pads. Or maybe the one giant messy list with lots of items crossed out and more tasks jammed onto the bottom of the list. You may even have a folder or two on your desk somewhere titled ASAP or URGENT. In it are "very important" tasks you need to get to. Except the folder has probably been buried on your desk for some time.

The problem with those lists is that they are disorganized, overwhelming, unreliable and impossible to prioritize.

The following is a simple plan to get your to-do list under control.

The Brain Dump

As David Allen says, "You can't be comfortable not doing something unless you know what it is you're not doing." But if your tasks are scattered about on several lists, it's almost certain something will fall through the cracks just because it's not on the list you're currently using.

With a brain dump, you gather all of your to do's in one spot. (Just to make sure we're in agreement on terminology, when I say "to do" I mean tasks and activities. The terms are interchangeable for the purposes here.)

Gather all of your lists and random scraps, and don't forget any electronic lists you may have started. This process should include personal to do's as well since this is a brain clearing exercise.

Sitting at your computer, start transferring all of the tasks onto one list.

I suggest using a two-column format illustrated here. You can download a template at https://www.mckcoaching.com/mmm-resources/

TO DO LIST
enter date here

SHORT RANGE

MARKETING
•
•
•

NOTES TO WRITE
•
•
•

SALES CALLS/PHONE CALLS
•
•
•

BOOKEEPING/FINANCIAL
•
•
•

PROSPECTING
•
•
•

WRITING/BLOG POSTS
•
•
•

PROPOSALS
•
•
•

VOLUNTEER COMMITMENTS
•
•

ERRANDS
•
•
•

PROFESSIONAL DEVELOPMENT
•
•
•

AT COMPUTER
•

You see that there are categories on this template. The ones shown are thought-starters. You'll likely need to change them to align better with your work.

As you're transferring all of the tasks to this document, don't get too caught up in the categories. If you're not sure which ones you need right now, it will become clearer as you go along.

As you're putting your to do's on the new document, other tasks may occur to you, so get them down, too. Toss the papers and notes as you capture the information from them.

Once all of the to do's are on the new document you can sort them by moving them around within their individual category.

There are three sections on the template: Short-Range, Long-Range and Perhaps.

The Short-Range list is for tasks you want to complete in the next two weeks or so. The Long-Range list is for tasks you definitely need to do but are due further out. The Perhaps list is for ideas and tasks that aren't definite yet, but you may choose to do them at some point. The Perhaps list is essentially a safe place to store ideas, so you don't worry about forgetting them.

You may have duplicate categories on your Short and Long-Range lists. And you see there are no categories at all on the Perhaps list. Remember that this template is to get you started. Adjust anything you like to make it work for you.

While you can choose to keep the document on your computer, unprinted, I prefer a printed copy. It may seem old school but it's what works for many. Maybe you're better off with print, too. It's tangible and that can often help with keeping your mind organized.

Print the entire document and now you have a multi-page hard copy list that includes all of your to do's.

It's refreshing isn't it? There is a sense of peace and yes, contentment, when you know that everything you need to do is captured in one secure place.

However, this is not the list you work from each day. Having to choose from your entire Short-Range list all day long would be challenging at best.

From your Short-Range list, you'll choose three—just three—tasks and put them on a separate sheet in the order you want/need to do them. This is the list you work from throughout the day.

With just three things on your list at any one time, you can quickly prioritize and reprioritize as necessary.

A Simple Process to Prioritize

I've said that you should only have three tasks on your immediate to-do list because it's so easy to prioritize three items. You'll do something first, second or third. Even if two things seem to have equal priority, one of them has to be chosen to do first or you'll multitask—and you know you don't want to do that.

This method also helps if a new task comes up that could throw off your plan. When you consider this new task you just need to decide if it needs to replace one of the three items currently on your list or if it can go onto your Short-Range, Long-Range or Perhaps list.

The new task can be a distracting bright shiny object if you don't think carefully about its true priority.

If you get seriously stuck trying to prioritize occasionally, you can use a Priority Ranking System to help you make decisions. It provides places to assess the urgency and value of each task and assign scores. The item with the highest score is your top priority. Access a dowloadable copy of the form on the resources page for this book. https://www.mckcoaching.com/mmm-resources/

Daily Focus Sheet

When your top three tasks are complete, you can go back and get three more tasks—or maybe fewer—dependent upon how much time you have left to work that day.

You can choose to jot those three tasks you pull off of your Short-Range list onto a legal pad. Or if you'd like something more all-encompassing, you can use a Daily Focus Sheet to focus your day. Download a copy of that here. https://www.mckcoaching. com/mmm-resources/

The Daily Focus Sheet has an area to write in your highest priority tasks from your Short-Range list—three at a time. There are also areas to note projects you need to keep top of mind, good things that happen during the day (moments where you experienced contentment perhaps), personal tasks you need to take care of, a reminder of your Preferred Stalling Technique (see Chapter Seven), and what technique or cueing device you'll use to focus if you wander into that PST. Plus, add a small section for random notes.

My assumption is that if you use the Daily Focus Sheet, it may be for only a short while. It's essentially a cueing device to help you put into practice the ideas featured on it. Once the process become more routine, you may not need the sheet to remind you of best practices.

You also may choose to create your own Daily Focus Sheet customized for your needs. Or you may want to use the Sheet as-is long-term. It's all okay. Just do what gets you optimal results.

Having a small, manageable list allows you to focus on your highest priority needs without seeing absolutely everything you have to do every time you glance at your list. Which, frankly, would be overwhelming and distracting.

Updating Your Lists

To-do lists are ever evolving and it's likely that soon after you printed your entire Brain Dump list, you thought of something else to add to it.

Instead of dashing back to your computer every time, just jot the task on the appropriate list. Yes, it will get messy as you cross out items and add new ones. But remember, your Short-Range list is for tasks you want to do in the next two weeks. So, every two weeks you'll be updating and refreshing all your lists.

Note on your calendar when you want to carve out time to update your lists. Maybe every other Friday afternoon. Your update process includes:

- Looking at your Perhaps list to see if anything has moved up in priority
- Looking at your Long-Range list and seeing what needs to be moved to Short-Range
- Deleting anything on any list that has been completed
- Typing in anything that was written in and isn't yet completed
- Printing out a fresh, clean copy of the new list
- Many people choose to keep their old lists in a file while others toss them. It's up to you.

This is a simple, mostly paper-based system to manage your to do's. Like everything else I develop, simplicity was at the forefront of my mind when I created it.

The Only To-Do List that Matters

Items on to-do lists tend to get treated as though they are all equally important. But they really aren't. If you look carefully at any list, you'll see things that:

- it would be nice to do
- I should do
- I would like to do
- I must do
- I may do someday
- I will do

- somebody else told me to do
- I am doing today

So, which of those lists is the most important? Some might say "Things I must do." But take filing taxes, for instance. Most people would put that on their "must do" list and yet some still might not do it before an extension is required.

The list that matters the most is the list of things you *are doing* today. If something doesn't ever get done, it should have been on one of those other lists.

The hundreds of potential tasks you think up are not going to go away—you're always going to be adding to one list or another. But you can make peace with those lists by wrapping your brain around your own reality, making conscious decisions about what you do, and then being okay with the things that don't get crossed off.

Capture To Dos On-the-Go

It's one thing to sit at your desk and think of tasks you need to get done and add them to your to-do list. But what do you do when you're going from place to place all day and yet still have to capture new tasks? You don't want to forget about them before you get back to the office.

The good news—and the bad news—is that you have a LOT of options:

- Phone app
- Notebook
- Moleskin
- Planner system
- Voice memo
- Spiral bound 3x5 cards

All of those can work. Where you get into trouble is if you use more than one of them. You end up losing track of tasks because no single on-the-go list is regularly used. A voice memo here, a sticky note there, tasks buried in meeting notes, reminders on scraps of paper.

The remedy is simple. Pick one.

Pick one app. Or one pen/paper option. Or capture everything via voice memo. You may even want to use a planner system with a tab specifically for to dos captured on-the-go. With one option chosen, you always know which option to use, and when you get back to the office you just have to review one source and transfer what you captured onto the appropriate section of your Brain Dump To-Do List.

Venue Shift

I coined the term Venue Shift for the period of time when you're leaving one place and arriving at another—like when you leave a meeting at a client office and arrive back at your own office. Those moments right when you get back can be a bit aimless. You might check email or straighten up your desk, perhaps chat with a co-worker. It's hard to get back into a good rhythm.

But with this to-do system you'll know exactly what to start on when you get back to your desk. Just glance at your list of three and tackle the next item.

Sure, you may be losing just a few minutes at a time, but those minutes add up. If you want to see how fast costs add up when you aren't using time purposefully, check out the Cost of Lost Focus Calculator on my website. The results are often staggering. Find a link to that Calculator here. https://www.mckcoaching.com/mmm-resources/

Tips to Make Your To-Do List Work for You

Give This Time

Setting up and using this system is new. It's not going to be comfortable and feel routine right away. Give it time. Resist the urge to abandon it for the bright, shiny, new option. Use it. Tweak it. Use it some more. Adjust it. Repeat.

Use Verbs

Items without a verb don't belong on a to-do list. For example, website, marketing plan, staff party, case study, office relocation—to name a few—are all items I've seen on to-do lists. Problem is, those are *projects*, not *tasks*, and second, there are no clear actions to take.

Every task that you need to complete should include a verb. For instance: call, meet, e-mail, schedule, plan, write, draft, compose, review, research, buy, price, compare, think about, look up, find, file, sort, purge, clean out.

And since I mentioned projects…

Differentiate Projects and Tasks

Does this scenario sound familiar?

The deadline looms for a significant project. Knowing it needs to get done and yet not having started on it yet creates a pervasive gnawing at your brain. The dread can go anywhere from a sense of unease to full blown panic.

The anxiety will diminish somewhat as soon as you get started, so you look at your schedule for a big chunk of time that you can set aside to focus on it.

Problem? A big chunk of time is exactly what you'll likely never get.

Deep down you already know this. Big chunks of time are like mirages. You can see them clearly in the distance, but they vanish as soon as you're upon them.

In order to get this project done, you'll have to break it down into manageable, do-able tasks. Define tasks which when dealt with one at a time move progress forward bit by bit to project completion.

In the 19 years that I've been helping clients with just such challenges, I consistently see an error which throws off the entire process and puts a roadblock in the path to getting things done.

That immobilizing error is that the tasks aren't broken down into small enough pieces.

Here's how to know if your pieces are small enough.

A task is one step. If an item on your task list includes more than one step, you have a sub-project, not a task. The following are one very basic example, and one that's more complex.

Basic Example

If you need to make a call and have the phone number handy, that phone call is a task. If you have to find the phone number (call this a speed bump) via quick research before you can make the call, that call is a project which includes the tasks of acquiring the number and then making the call. If you have "make the call" on your task list and don't have the number available, you'll continually bypass the task and take care of other—perhaps less important—tasks that don't have speed bumps involved.

This happened to a client of mine who was so busy he just kept passing over the phone call task, not consciously aware of the reason. By taking a second to examine why the task kept lingering, he realized not having the phone numbers was the speed bump. As soon as he got his assistant to put the numbers on his desk, he made the calls immediately.

Sounds like a "duh" moment, but it's not. I see it all the time and it's because we're moving so fast.

Complex Example

Big projects obviously need to be broken down. For instance, if you need to create or update a business plan, that's a complex project with many tasks. Breaking down a complex project into manageable tasks is your first task—and one most people skip!

For the business plan project, you might have as your second task (after breaking down the project) "find sample of business plan" followed by "review sample business plan" and then "draft outline of business plan." With the draft outline in hand, any subprojects can be defined and those can be broken down into tasks as well.

It's deceptively simple, but not easy—which I know from countless experiences with clients. Working as a team, we get down to the very core of each task to make certain what's on the task list is do-able as a task, and that tasks are in the proper order.

As you break down your project, the question to ask for each item is whether you'll be able to complete that task in one step and in the order you've placed it in the plan. If you can't complete it in one step, it must be broken down further. And the order of tasks must be listed in the order you can complete them. Or as one of my more humorous clients puts it, "socks first, then shoes."

Being faced with a complex project can create anxiety, but by utilizing this process you're better poised to avoid overwhelm.

Breaking down your projects prevents you from having a breakdown!

Narrow Your Focus

If you have many, perhaps even dozens of projects you want to be working on right now, you're in good company.

Problem is, having all those projects on your mind simultaneously erodes focus, increases stress and reduces productivity. When you dilute your focus on too many projects it's difficult to stick with any one of them long enough to make significant progress. It's okay to have many projects you want to accomplish, but not okay to be actively working on too many at a time.

Better to choose the three most important or highest priority projects and put your attention there. The other projects don't have to be abandoned, just keep track of them on your Perhaps list and work on them when the time is right.

Projects are like rolls of toilet paper. You only need one within arm's reach in every bathroom and the rest stored away. When you're ready for more, it's easy to replace that roll.

This rule of three doesn't apply to client work. The projects I'm referring to are initiatives that more likely fall under working "on" the business. Things like developing new products or services, reworking some part of the business infrastructure, e.g., marketing or technology, or planning a move or acquisition.

The Tasks You'll Never Do

Think about the to-do lists you've created in the past. What do they all have in common?

Some things on each list got done and, almost assuredly, some things didn't.

There are times when you pass over a task again and again, always choosing something other than that task. Think back to a time when you had an item sit on your to-do list for a long while. At some point did you realize the task no longer needed to be done?

Perhaps so much time passed that it wasn't relevant any longer. Or someone else took care of it. Or maybe circumstances changed, and it just didn't need to be done.

What are the consequences for you not doing a particular task? In many cases, not getting it done registers barely a blip in your life or work. It goes back to all the different types of items we talked about earlier in "The Only To-Do List That Matters" section.

Don't beat yourself up for the things you don't actually do on your list. Just writing it down doesn't make it mandatory.

I truly don't say this in a morbid way, but in all likelihood, we're going to die with things still on our to-do lists! That's really okay. What that says is that you strived to the end. I plan to do that.

If you expect that every task on all your lists must be done, you forfeit your chance at contentment. Instead, take a moment to experience the contentment when you do cross something off.

Schedule Meetings for Maximum Efficiency

Meetings can be soul-sucking, mind-numbing exercises in triviality robbing you of quality time to do real, productive work. But whether they are or not, you're probably not going to be able to get out of them—at least not all of them. Here are a few tips for managing your calendar so meetings don't destroy your efforts to get things done.

The tips here aren't startling news, but busy people—like you— are often moving so fast that time isn't taken to implement ideas like these. Slow down just a couple of minutes to think about and execute these ideas and your schedule will be more manageable.

Schedule travel time on your calendar

Schedule adequate time to make the trip. If you're driving to the meeting, calculate realistically how long the trip should take from your office to the meeting room, including getting out of or into garages, traffic at that time of day, etc. Ideally you want to be wherever you're headed at least a few minutes ahead of time. If you set alarms for your departure time, you can avoid that momentary freak-out when you realize you were so focused in thought that now you're leaving late and will *be* late.

Stack off-site appointments in multiples

If your business requires meetings over breakfast, lunch, coffee or in other people's offices, take one day of your week or month and schedule as many as possible in that one day. Ideally, you can choose a coffee shop or restaurant and have all your meetings in the same place and people will come to you. It's thoughtful to choose a convenient location to many areas of town to make it easy for others to get to you.

There are so many benefits to this. One, you save all the travel time driving from meeting to meeting. Two, you can book appointments back to back so meetings won't run long because your next appointment shows up. Three, you can introduce your current meeting partner to your next meeting partner, thereby making a new connection for both of them. And four, if someone cancels at the last minute, you can use the found time to catch up on other work. Always bring your laptop or some work you can do in the event of a cancellation.

I had client who's in a business where everyone wants to meet and "pick his brain." It's good for his business to have those meetings, and besides, he's a very sharp and generous guy. We decided that he should designate one day and park himself at the coffee shop. When people ask for a meeting, he has a day and time to offer them. It's a very productive day for him because he's not driving all over town many times a month to have the meetings. Inevitably someone has something come up and can't make the meeting, but it's okay with him because he gets an extra hour and can cross a few things off his task list.

Meet virtually and avoid travel time entirely

Take advantage of Facetime, Skype, ZOOM, or GoTo Meeting and save yourself the drive time. Sometimes being face-to-face is just better relationship building and/or fosters clearer communication, but you don't have to be in the same room to do that.

Always have an agenda

It doesn't matter how basic it is, you need to know why you're having this meeting. If you don't know that, how will you determine if it's a good use of your time?

The agenda could be as simple as a single purpose, e.g., learning more about the other person's work to see if a business relationship is beneficial for you both. Even with that type of meeting, you need to go in knowing what you want to learn before you part ways to determine if another meeting at some point makes sense.

For group meetings, it's vital to have an agenda. Follow it meticulously to stay on point. Rambling meetings are appreciated by no one. Use the "parking lot" method when people bring up items that aren't on the agenda. Literally write the topic on a flip chart or white board and at the end of the meeting make a plan for deciding when to discuss those items.

Efficiently run meetings are useful, quick and less costly. At minimum, people may dread *your* meetings less than others.

Schedule meetings for 50 minutes instead of one hour

I schedule my client coaching calls this way. This allows for a 10-minute buffer since many appointments are scheduled on the hour or half hour. For your meetings, those 10 minutes can be used to make notes about what you may have committed to do or what follow-up is required. You can also take a couple of minutes to regroup and shift your focus to the agenda of the next meeting.

Schedule even shorter meetings

If attendees are focused enough, could you accomplish in just 15 minutes what you need to get done? Can you have the meeting standing up? Every minute you save during a busy day is a minute you can put to better use, even if that use is coming to a complete stop to clear your mind and reassess your priorities.

Block time on your calendar

If other people have access to your calendar and can book meetings whenever it appears you're available, make certain you block out time for your most important tasks so those times are unavailable. If a meeting is critical enough and you appear unavailable, the organizer will call you to see if this blocked time can be opened up. You can determine, on a case by case basis, whether the meeting or your important task takes precedence.

Micro-Scheduling

Micro-scheduling is adding those "smallest possible steps" directly to your calendar so you'll be more committed to doing them. Tasks you might overlook stand a *much* better chance of getting done when you block time for them.

Once scheduled, treat those calendar entries like you would any other appointment made with a human being. You don't blow those off, do you? Be as committed and respectful to the commitments you make to yourself as you are to the ones you make to other people.

Some of these may be second nature to you and as such don't require scheduling. But, if you find yourself wanting or meaning to do these things and they just keep not getting done or done with enough regularity, schedule them on your calendar and intensify your commitment.

- Making sales calls—Even though this is a vitally important revenue-generating task, it can often get overlooked. Micro-schedule your sales time and commit to it no matter what.
- Reading—Journals, newspapers or books. For business or pleasure. No matter what you're reading, the benefits are great. People who read are better writers and better thinkers.
- Meditating/Breathing/Stretching—Days are busy and rushed so it never feels like a natural time to do this. Make your "natural" time the time you planned.
- Thinking about your business—This requires quiet time and isn't easily checked off of your to do list. Great business ideas surface when you quiet your mind. Scheduling 30 minutes of thinking time will usually boil down to 10 minutes of solid business creativity once your mind stops racing.

- Exercise—Unless your sport is already a part of your regular routine, you're more likely to get the workout in if you commit to it on your calendar. Carve out the time in advance instead of seeing what time you have left to squeeze it in.
- Decluttering—Stuff comes into your space with very little effort but getting rid of things takes planning and decision-making. Put it off for too long and you're overrun with stuff, which ultimately clutters your brain, too.
- Writing notes by hand—A great batch activity. If you want to connect with someone, sending a personal note by mail makes you stand out and is lovely to receive. Have your supplies handy and dash off several at a time.
- Any task you dislike—Thinning out email, filing, reconciling your bank account, completing expense reports, etc. If you don't like doing them, you'll find a reason not to do them. Schedule and commit to a time to handle administrivia and note specifically what tasks you'll do during the time allotted.

Micro-scheduling your entire day doesn't work. Life and business are so fluid that in most jobs you need to be nimbler than that. Use micro-scheduling judiciously. When you do, you'll be more likely to adhere to your micro-scheduled commitments that appear on your schedule like appointments, not just tasks.

CHAPTER SEVEN

Putting Off Procrastination

W e've all been there. Putting things off that need to be done. It can be a big thing like finding a better job or getting in shape. Or a medium-sized thing like writing a proposal or cleaning out the garage. Or even a small thing like scheduling an appointment with your physician.

You know you'll feel better if you get started, or better yet, get it done. But, instead of launching into it, you either busy yourself with relatively unimportant but less distasteful tasks or make 38 excuses for why starting later will be just fine.

I don't believe you procrastinate because you're a perfectionist, and research backs me up. Mostly we put off doing things we don't like, don't know how to do, or believe we need more time to do than we currently have.

Many of the suggestions in this Chapter are only subtly different. They are almost entirely focused on thinking differently and overcoming the powerful urge to wait until later. Read through the entire chapter looking for the ideas that resonate with you. If you've tried something before and it didn't work, try it again. We change and grow, and what wasn't the right thing in the past may be just what you need to hear now.

You're Doubling Up on Your Anxiety

Consider this: Even though you're putting something off because you don't want to do it or it's not fun or doesn't make you feel good, *not* doing the thing isn't fun, either. Nor does *not* doing it make you feel good or make you any happier.

So, by procrastinating you DOUBLE your lousy feelings. You still have the dread of the project or task, but now you also have the guilt from procrastinating.

The Illogical Logic of Procrastination

In the back of your mind, you know that task you're putting off is lurking out there. Perhaps you don't focus on it constantly. Stretches of time pass without it clogging your brain. But then suddenly the realization hits that you still must get it done. Rather like when you wake up in great mood and suddenly remember that today is your root canal.

Here's a way to think…and do…differently.

When the urge strikes to procrastinate, ask yourself this question: "If I wait two days to complete this, will the task be less unpleasant then?"

Most often the answer is, "no." The task is still not going to be something you want to do. The passage of time doesn't have a positive influence.

For the sake of this example, let's assume the unpleasant task will take an hour to complete. Which means if you just do it now, you'll be miserable for an hour. But by putting it off for two days you can now be miserable for an hour plus the two days you spent dreading it.

Which option makes more sense now?

Hoping It Will Be Easier Later

A client had a challenge at work and it could only be fixed by having what was likely going to be an uncomfortable conversation. While he knew it had to be addressed, he'd been putting it off longer than he liked.

Sounds normal. When you have to do something unpleasant, the natural inclination is to put it off. But my client figured something out. He realized that he was putting it off in the hope that he'd figure out a way to make it easier. He admitted that was highly unlikely.

When you procrastinate, maybe your expectations aren't so optimistic as to think the task will eventually be "easy." Perhaps you just want it to be less hideous, or uncomfortable, or boring, or time-consuming.

But if that thing will continue to be hideous, uncomfortable, boring or time-consuming, just get going on it and get it behind you.

Happy Now or Happy for the Long Haul

Every day, in every moment, you have the opportunity to make decisions about how to spend your minutes. You can choose to do things that make you happy in the moment and you can choose things that make you happy over the long haul.

Here are some "Happy Now vs Happy for the Long Haul" examples:

Sitting on the couch watching TV vs. Using that time to read a book or perhaps start *writing* your own book

Shopping for stuff you don't need vs. Donating the money you would have spent to your favorite charity

Aimlessly surfing the web vs. Getting out of the house for a walk or a run

Complaining with friends about how you hate your job vs. Doing some inner work to discover what you'd *like* to be doing, or updating your resumè

Avoiding the person who wronged you and harboring anger towards them vs. Having a thoughtful conversation with that person about how you view what happened to see if you can work it out

In the cases above, the top choices in the pairs aren't as much about creating happiness as they are avoidance techniques or just mindless actions. The bottom choices in the pairs, which require stopping the procrastination, take an extra push to get going, but pay off in long-term personal satisfaction.

But you know that, right?

Sometimes the unpleasant situation wins the procrastination war because doing something about it seems too daunting. And it's true that starting a big project or making a change in behavior can be challenging. That whole "body at rest tends to stay at rest" has proven to be powerfully true.

What if you take just *one* step in the direction that seems so challenging and see what that does for you?

It feels powerful and invigorating to finally get in motion. When was the last time you felt all puffed up about accomplishing something that came easily to you? You get real satisfaction from stretching, from pushing yourself, sometimes in small ways and sometimes far beyond what you thought you could do.

Remember, that Striving is on the top half of the State of Mind Model. Striving is a vital part of your happiness and it's work. Work that's worth it.

Preferred Stalling Technique

In Chapter Five we talked about Preparation vs. Procrastination and I shared a list of things that more than likely fall into the latter category. Let's take this idea a bit further to personalize it for you.

When you don't want to do something what do you tend to do to put off doing that dreaded task? How about one or more of these:

- Check email
- Clean out email
- Get on social media
- Grab a snack
- Watch TV
- Surf the web
- Shop online
- Chat with a co-worker
- Clean out files
- For those who work from home, any domestic chore
- Other _____

Whatever you chose is your Preferred Stalling Technique (PST). It's a time sinkhole.

Doing these tasks at the wrong time isn't good for your state of mind, because you know you're stalling even as you feel helpless to stop it. Worse, you feel either more overwhelmed or hopelessly behind when you go back to thinking about important work.

Monitor yourself. Use your cueing device to keep you focused. When you see yourself drifting into your PST, take action to redirect yourself to a more productive path.

Catastrophizing a Task

Sometimes a task ends up not being as awful as you predicted it might be. Once you're into it for five minutes, you find it was no big deal at all. Now procrastinating for two days goes from being ridiculous to *spectacularly* ridiculous.

Take a moment or two and think about a task you've been putting off. Something that you think is going to be difficult, or take forever, or be scary to do, or has the potential to make someone unhappy with you if you don't do it.

Got one? Good. Now I'll tell you mine. It's okay if you laugh at how dumb this is. One, because I deserve it. Two, because I'll probably never know you did.

I had never put air in my own tires because I didn't know how. Wasn't sure how much air should go in there. Was afraid the tire might explode if I did it wrong, etc. So, when a tire was low it became a much bigger deal than it needed to be. I would hope that I only needed air whenever some other service was being done.

That changed one day when I noticed that my tire was frighteningly low. My father-in-law called it to my attention and I chose to ignore it for all the reasons I mentioned above—and then I forgot about it. More time passed, and it was so low I was quite worried as I drove to a station with an air machine. But after decades of driving and never putting air in my own tires, even when not doing so was also stressful, I managed it.

And it was no big deal. Nothing exploded. The air machine was user-friendly. All those years of all that worry. For what?!

Hopefully, whatever the thing is that you thought of at the beginning of this section hasn't been bugging you for decades. But it's quite possible that it, too, will not be nearly as big a deal as you think it is right now.

What IS a big deal is all the mental energy spent thinking about it instead of actually doing it—thereby making it worse than it ever had to be.

EXERCISE

Take that task you chose at the beginning of this section and start on it. If it's a tough conversation, reach out and schedule a meeting or a cup of coffee. If it's a task as small as putting air in tires, just go do it. The book will be here when you get back.

Right now. Write down what you've been putting off and how you feel about it. Just pour it all out. Then, go take that first step or complete the task. Then come back here and write down how you feel now. Pull up this "after" feeling next time you see yourself veering toward catastrophizing.

Endlessly Gathering Data

Many years ago, when exercise videos were a new thing, my sister and I developed what we thought was a brilliant plan to make sure we bought the most effective videos. We didn't want to spend money on them only to find out they didn't offer a solid workout or were boring.

We carefully researched options and rented the exercise videos we thought had serious potential. Then we watched them while we sat on the couch eating Cheetos and sour cream.

Our plan was severely flawed.

It's a perfect description of the trap we all can fall into: Gathering data instead of actually doing anything.

Gathering more information is a procrastination technique disguised as preparation.

Sometimes you legitimately need more information in order to move forward. But sometimes you don't. Ask yourself, "In this situation do I need more information, or do I just need to take action on what I have?"

Being Controlled by Your But

Life can be overbooked, overwhelming and stressful. As we've already discovered together, you have enormous control over just how much you get done. Yet you may not exercise that control as much as you could.

Do any of these statements sound familiar?

- I want to work on this project today, *but* I really need a chunk of time to devote to it.
- I should follow up with this prospect, *but* I'll knock out these other quick tasks and then I'll make the call.
- I've been meaning to get this office organized, *but* I just don't have the time.
- I need to make a plan for each day, *but* I really have to hit the ground running just to keep up.
- I know I shouldn't check e-mail first thing in the morning, but I'm afraid if I don't, I'll miss something terribly important.

Follow-through is pretty much a black and white thing. You either do or you don't. Doing the thing you say you'll do gets results you're happier about. Not doing the thing you say you'll do and coming up with a "good" excuse for why you didn't do it leads to feeling unaccomplished, frustrated, overwhelmed, and worse, you forfeit your opportunity to experience contentment.

Be mindful of your but. When you say, "but", is it just an excuse?

Talking Sense into Yourself

When you really, truly don't want to do something, tell yourself so. Out loud. Explain to yourself why you want or need to put this off.

- I don't like this task.
- I don't want to do it.
- It's boring.
- I don't know how to do it.
- I shouldn't have to do this.
- What if I do it and the result is lousy?
- I don't have enough time to do it.
- I'll get started later.

The key to this exercise isn't in the talking, but in the listening. Listen to yourself as if the voice were coming from some other person sharing those reasons with you. Maybe a co-worker or colleague is saying them. Perhaps a child or teenager. If someone you care about said those statements to you, how would you respond? Play both roles. The Procrastinating Self and the Wiser Self.

On the next page is a chart that illustrates what this conversation can sound like.

PROCRASTINATING SELF	WISER SELF
I don't like this task.	Just because you don't like it doesn't mean you don't have to do it. Get on it.
I don't want to do it.	We all have to do things we don't want to do sometimes. Like going to funerals or the dentist. You can't wait until you *want* to do it because you'll never want to do it. May as well get started now.
It's boring.	And it will be just as boring later. At which time, by the way, you will have made it even worse by wasting hours, days or weeks dreading it. Now there's some fun. It's just a task—get it over with.
I don't know how to do it?	What part of the task is stumping you? Let's get you the help you need.
I shouldn't have to do this.	Maybe you're right. Who *should* have to do this? Can you delegate it? Pay someone else to do it?
What if I do it and the result is lousy?	What makes you think it will be lousy? Do you have a history of doing lousy work?
I don't have enough time to do it.	How much time will it take? Can you break the project down into do-able chunks? Let's do that.
I'll get started later.	What are you doing now that's more important than this task?

See how it works? You end up having both sides of the conversation and can rationally see that the excuses don't have much validity.

Just Five Minutes

Get out the kitchen timer we talked about in Chapter Five. Set it for five minutes. Just five minutes. Do whatever tiny piece of work you can do in that five minutes. When you hear the ding indicating time is up you can move on to something else. But what may happen, is that once you get started you'll keep going and get more done than you thought.

Do the Small Thing

You have a project to do and the deadline is looming. Or worse, the deadline is self-imposed and therefore fluid. But, completing this project is important and it's gnawing away at your brain. You're motivated because the boss is breathing down your neck (negative motivation) or will perhaps generate revenue for you (positive motivation). But you're also a bit paralyzed.

What to do?

Do one infinitesimally small task. Do one, tiny little thing that will move you forward. Don't worry about whether your motivation is strong enough to keep you going on to the next task. Just do this one thing related to the project.

Tiny is easier to accomplish than big. And surprisingly, paralysis wanes with any movement forward.

Seven Second Syndrome™

Right now, before you read the rest of this post, stop and count to seven the way you used to as a kid: One one thousand, two one thousand, and so on.

Done? Good.

Did it seem like a long time? Short amount of time?

To me, counting it out always makes it feel like more time than I imagine it to be. Whether it went quickly or more slowly than you may have assumed, it's pretty astounding what can go through your mind in seven seconds. No?

And that's why sometimes you need to take action before those seven seconds kick in. These times include the moment you decide to:

- Get up and go for that walk or run
- Start writing that proposal
- Make the sales calls
- Practice the presentation
- Start pulling together the tax papers
- Plow through the stack of filing
- Say "I'm sorry"

I call this the Seven Second Syndrome. In those seven seconds you can come up with a myriad of excuses for why doing that thing later makes sense. Or why doing something else, even if it might not be as important, is a better choice.

Don't fall prey to the Seven Second Syndrome! Beat the seven seconds to the punch and just get started before your brain tries to talk you out of it.

Seven Second Save

There are instances when waiting the seven seconds is the smart thing to do. This is called the Seven Second Save. Instead of lurching ahead with what you're thinking of doing, count to seven. Here are some occasions when you'll be glad you practiced some restraint:

- When the last half of the enormous dessert is sitting in front of you (do you really want the whole thing?)
- When you've just drafted an angry email and are about to hit send
- When you're about to say something in a conversation that you won't be able to take back
- When you're being asked to volunteer for something. Rather than blurting out the answer the other person wants to hear and then ending up with an unmanageable schedule and the stress that goes along with it.

Seven seconds sounds like an insignificant amount of time. But, look at the difference it can make!

Paralyzed by Possibility

Have you ever had many options and been stumped trying to choose the best one? Some people love coming up with ideas. Their brains work in creativity overtime. They can go so many directions and all of them can seem like viable, worthy options.

But for others of us there is a big downside.

In a book called *The Paradox of Choice: Why More is Less,* the author, Barry Schwartz says:

"...we assume that more choice means better options and greater satisfaction. But beware of excessive choice: choice overload can

make you question the decisions you make before you even make them, it can set you up for unrealistically high expectations, and it can make you blame yourself for any and all failures."

Having too many ideas is overwhelming. I call it Paralyzed by Possibility.

If this sounds like you, limit your input. Don't over research. Tell others up front that it's problematic for you to have too many choices.

I share this information with people I hire to help me. Part of their value to me is to pare down what I need to know so I can make better, easier decisions.

You Had the Power All Along

How are losing weight and overcoming procrastination the same?

Both are impossible.

Just kidding. It just seems that way sometimes.

If I asked you what you need to do, generally, to lose weight what would you answer?

Eat less and move more, right? It's pretty simple.

Yet there are over 122,000 books out there sharing wisdom about how to shed those pounds. That's because people want a different answer than the one they have, even if the answer they already have would lead them to the result they want. The hope is that maybe this new diet will be easier. Maybe this plan won't require a change in eating *and* exercise habits. Or maybe the changes will seem so small as to be do-able while still resulting in big weight loss.

At the same time, you know that at the root of it, a plan and discipline are required. If you make the right choices more often than you make choices that lead you away from your goal, you'll eventually weigh what you want to weigh. It doesn't take reading 122,000 books to know that, but that may not stop you from wishing there was an easier way.

Search Amazon for "overcoming procrastination" and there are about 2,642 results. In those results you'll find many reasons why you procrastinate, what's happening in the procrastinator's brain, types of procrastination, processes to follow to stop procrastinating, tips, charts, methods and tricks—all to help you get off your bum and do the work.

But at the root of it is that at some point you just have to do it. You have to stop wringing your hands or turning to email or justifying why you should do it later or never do it at all—and just do it.

With losing weight, it is important to find exercise that you enjoy—or at least don't dread—and food that satisfies you. Eating well and staying active isn't a short-term deal. If you want to stay fit you have to keep it up, so it just makes sense to make it all as pleasant as possible. Consequently, the information you get in a few of those 122,000 books is, of course, helpful if you learn things that will make your journey to a healthy body enjoyable.

Same thing with overcoming procrastination. I'm able to share a great deal of information about how to tackle and conquer the tasks that languish on your to-do list. There is huge value in the tips, processes and mindsets I share that help pave the way to getting things done and feeling accomplished instead of putting things off and feeling guilty. And in the end, it's you who makes the decision in any given moment to get started rather than delay another day.

It's like Dorothy and the ruby slippers. You have had the power all along.

CHAPTER EIGHT

Managing Stress

B ack in Chapter Two I talked about the myth that next week will be less crazy than this week. Unless you're going to be sitting in a beach chair looking at the ocean next week, it's probably going to be equally busy for you next week, even if you don't see it coming right now.

If busy is the rule and not the exception, stress is part of the deal.

You don't need to get rid of all your stress. You need to reduce it or eliminate some of it by getting better at choosing and focusing. Some stress, you just need to manage.

This chapter is all about developing the mindset and practices to help you manage the stress in your life.

I don't expect that you'll do all of these at once. Some of them may already be a part of your routine. Terrific. Keep them up. Others may be familiar and interesting to you but not part of your life. Choose one at a time that resonates with you and begin fitting it into your day.

You may want to add them to your Quick Start or Wrap Up checklist to help you remember to do them. Or use a cueing device, like we discussed in Chapter Five.

Managing stress isn't a thing you check off your bucket list. Like physical health, mental health takes daily attention, even if you only have time for a smidgen of attention on it on some days.

Here are the ideas, mindsets and practices I know can impact you in remarkably positive ways.

Slow Down

Schedules are packed, and deadlines are tight. Combined, you feel like you need to speed up to jam everything in. Pay attention to what happens to your body and brain when you speed up.

In some cases, the adrenaline will be a plus, but often it's not. And in fact, speed sometimes does more harm than good. Take a breath and slow down. Here are eight reasons why you should reduce your pace:

1. **You'll be a better listener**—It's easy to get thinking so fast that you move on from what's being said to somewhere further along in the conversation. Maybe thinking about what you're going to say or just wishing the other person would get on with it. That pretty much makes for a lousy listener. If you don't have time for a conversation, say so. And if you're having a discussion, slow your brain down and stay in the moment.

2. **You'll get more of the right things done**—If you launch into the workday without planning, your default task is probably dealing with email. And you know that once you get sucked into email, hours can disappear with little to show for it. Slow down and work your plan.

3. **You'll have less to apologize for**—When somebody pushes your buttons, whether intentionally or not, your amygdala—responsible for your fight, flight, freeze or fold response—kicks in first. If you act in that moment, you may regret it. It's the very reason to write the angry email but wait until the next day to send it, when your more rational brain

(prefrontal cortex) will give you better advice. Hopefully, you delete that nasty email instead.

4. **You'll avoid wasting time**—How many times have you agonized and strategized about a problem that either never materialized or ended up getting fixed without your intervention? All that time and energy spent for nothing. Slow down and think about whether you really need to deal with this problem right now. Some people who thrive on variety and excitement may even be focusing on the problem because it's more interesting than a more important task. That sound familiar?

5. **You'll save money**—For many, buying is fun. The research, the actual purchase, the receiving can all be enjoyable. There's a bit of a dopamine hit associated with getting anything new. But that can be where the good feeling ends. The wanting can be more fun than the actual having. When the rush goes away, you focus on something else to research and buy in order to get that feeling back. If you think you need to buy something, write it down on a list or tear out the ad and keep it in a folder that you can look at in a week or a month. See if you still want/need it then.

6. **You'll produce higher quality work**—That familiar saying about "not having enough time to do it right but having enough time to do it over" is familiar because it happens all the time. Contrary to what many say, you don't really do your best work at the last minute. You produce whatever you can manage at the last minute and then try to convince yourself that it's really good.

7. **You'll be more considerate**—Moving too fast can make you want to finish other people's sentences, which is annoying,

especially when you finish it incorrectly. You also may miss social cues that are opportunities to show empathy or be courteous. I was in a meeting with a very fast-moving person. The way the conversation was going was getting less and less comfortable, even less tolerable, to me. But because the speaker was moving ahead so quickly, I'm almost certain my discomfort wasn't noticed. You can slow down in small ways. Hold the elevator for a co-worker even though it sets you back a few seconds. Offer to help someone struggling with a heavy load (either workload or literally a heavy box). Slow down and truly notice the people around you. Step in.

8. **You'll be safer**—Multitasking behind the wheel is disastrous. Same for speeding. Get in an accident or get a speeding ticket and see just how much time was "saved."

Be Mindful

Whatever you're doing, be fully aware and focused in that moment. Taking your first sip of coffee? Enjoy the warmth of the cup and the aroma, as well as the taste. Composing an email? Tune out everything else and focus on just that one task. Speaking with a colleague? Give that person your full attention.

Call it whatever you like: focus, mindfulness, being present. Having those calm moments makes a huge difference in how your workday goes, and frankly, how your life goes.

Breathe

Studies have shown that many people unconsciously hold their breath while typing and reading email. Linda Stone, a former Apple executive, calls this "email apnea." No wonder we're stressed by email! We're starved for oxygen!

Breathe to fill up your belly, not to fill your upper chest and shoulders. With each breath, take in enough air to expand your belly and with each exhale, expel as much breath as you can, pulling in your belly to extract every bit.

When you feel like you're spinning out of control mentally, do what I call the 5-5-5-5. Inhale for a count of five, hold it for a count of five and exhale to a count of five. Do it five times. Try it right now. Feel the difference?

Meditate

Meditating is truly nothing more than focusing on your breathing. For many years, I didn't meditate because I was afraid I wasn't doing it right. I also thought I had to clear my head, which was impossible. You don't need to clear your head—just acknowledge the thought and let it go. Refocus on your breath. You may need to do this hundreds of times in a session and that's okay!

Try this. Sit on the floor with your legs loosely crossed, or if you want back support, sit in a chair with your feet flat on the floor. Close your eyes or if you prefer, keep them open, focused a few feet in front of you.

I recommend a free app called Insight Timer which has hundreds of meditation options for any situation. With it, you don't have to look at a clock to see how long you've meditated. Just set the timer and a lovely bell sounds when time is up.

Relieve Tension

Right now, do a body scan and see where you might be experiencing tension. Your jaw? Face? Shoulders? When you drive, do you have a death grip on the steering wheel? Tension creeps in even when you don't feel like you're under stress.

Start noticing where you hold tension and focus on relaxing it away. This is another great time for a cueing device. Even a brightly colored sticky note that says "Quick Body Scan" or "Relax" will remind you to check tension levels and purposefully relax.

Stretch

So much of the workday can be spent immobilized staring at a computer screen. That tension we talked about above can lead to overall tightness when you're immobile for long periods of time. Throughout the day, raise and lower shoulders, do some head rolls, bend forward while sitting or standing, raise your arms over your head, do some side stretches.

Walk

It doesn't matter where you work, you can take five minutes and walk. Inside your building, around your parking lot, down the street in your neighborhood. Short breaks are uplifting and good for the body and mind. A walk will get your blood flowing and improve your brain function. If you can walk a dog, all the better. Pups are wonderful for reducing your stress.

Notice Nature

This can be purposeful or on the fly. Driving to work or walking by a window, pay attention to whatever nature you see. Having lunch, pick a seat where you can see outside, or better yet, sit outside. Listen to the sounds, smell the scents. Put a live plant or fresh flowers on your desk. Even for a few seconds, take in whatever nature falls into your line of sight.

Listen to Music

Choose some music to suit your mood—or perhaps to change it. Listen to soothing music to reduce tension, upbeat music to re-energize you, or your current favorite song to lift your spirits.

Declutter

Take a few minutes and clear off a corner of your desk that's been piling up or a drawer that has over-accumulated stuff. Getting rid of clutter feels good. Completing even a small project can have residual positive mental effects for days. I remember once cleaning out our junk drawer at home and it gave me moments of contentment every time I opened the drawer—for months!

Hydrate

If you are tired or think you're hungry, you may just be getting dehydrated.

Use a water bottle and a handful of rubber bands. For example, if you want to drink 64 oz. of water a day and you have a 16 oz. container, put four rubber bands around the top half of the bottle. Every time you empty the bottle, move a rubber band down to the bottom half of the bottle. That way you'll be able to visually track how much you've had to drink.

Always drink water as a first option before you go for the snack or caffeine. You may be able to stave off the craving for afternoon sugar or coffee.

Eat Well

I'm not a nutritionist, so will keep my thoughts here simple. You wouldn't expect your car to run well if you filled it with crappy gas or never changed the oil. Your body is the same. Fill it with lousy, empty calorie foods and it's not going to run at peak performance. If you're tired, a big cookie or candy bar in the afternoon won't kill you, but it's not going to do you many favors, either. (See the Stretch, Walk, Hydrate and Nap tips for better options.)

From personal experience I can tell you that eating less crud and more lean protein, fresh fruits and vegetables has had a mind-blowing impact on my ability to think, the quality of my sleep, and overall how I feel—in a very positive way. You don't have to go vegan—just make better choices now and then and you'll feel a difference.

Nap

I'm an expert napper. I come from a long-line of experienced nappers, including my mom who had five kids under nine years old. She called it "resting my eyes." My husband, never a napper before he met me, has taken to it like a champ.

It used to be nappers were considered slackers, and maybe some still wrongly think so. But early in my career, with a job that required much after 5:00 p.m. work with volunteers and hosting civic/social events, naps gave me the energy to keep going during extra-long work days.

A poll taken in 2011 by the National Sleep Foundation found that 43% of people don't get enough sleep. Tired people are clearly less effective people. Tired people who can't or won't nap usually resort to sugar or caffeine to keep going, and neither are good choices. They give a quick burst of energy, but also the inevitable plummet. And in a double whammy, the extra sugar also helps pack on pounds which saps energy.

Thankfully, more and more companies are understanding that rested employees are productive employees and are making accommodations for nappers. The Huffington Post has two (perhaps three by now) nap rooms for employees. Nationwide Planning Associates' New Jersey office has a nap room with a recliner where one employee at a time can grab a catnap.

If you want to try napping at work in an office environment, you'll need to make certain management is on board, so when your phone goes to voice mail and you're found snoozing, you don't have HR adding this performance tidbit to your permanent record.

If you're lucky enough to work for a company with a nap room, bully for you. But if not, your own office works, too. Keep a yoga mat behind your door so you can stretch out on the floor. You can also scrunch down in your chair and use a guest chair to prop up your feet.

If you work from home, you can also try the floor or perhaps the couch but don't get too comfortable.

Here are the rules about comfort: Lie on your back. No side-sleeping. And no blankets. Conditions for napping during work hours are not as cozy as a Saturday afternoon nap or bedtime sleeping. Napping is for when you're exhausted but have to keep going. Even with minimal comfort, if you're tired enough to need a nap, you'll fall asleep.

Once you've dozed off, you'll automatically wake up after 15-20 minutes. That's your cue to get up, stretch and get back to work. No exceptions! Going back to sleep after that initial waking will just leave you feeling groggy and disoriented when you finally do get up. Too long a nap is almost as bad as no nap.

You'll be amazed at the extra mental energy you'll have.

Trust me on this. I'm an expert.

Vacation

Take your vacation for criminy's sake!

Many people have a tough time either taking vacation or disconnecting from work while on vacation.

You may worry that something will blow up while you're gone. Or you think if you can just work a little bit every day, you'll avoid being too overwhelmed when you get back.

But keep this in mind:

Being busy feels important. Being needed is rewarding. If you're receiving a constant stream of communications to which you MUST respond, that must mean you're necessary.

In reality, you're necessary even without being that busy or constantly connected. You know that.

You owe it to yourself and your family (if you have one) to take your vacation and be fully present during that time. You'll deliver better work if you let yourself decompress and relax.

Disconnect

Occupying your attention with a laptop or smartphone is just easy. It's habit. Let your brain have a rest. Just sit. Let your mind go wherever it goes. If you're really attached to your electronic device, start slow. Put it away for 15 or 30 minutes. It may feel stressful at first. FOMO (Fear of Missing Out.)

But what might you be missing out on by spending so much time looking at a screen? People who care about you and hope you care about them. That's what.

Go on a Media Fast

A vacation is a perfect time for a media fast, though you'll benefit from one anytime. Turn off the television and the radio. Stay away from newspapers and avoid online news sources for whatever amount of time you can manage. Put your smartphone in a drawer. Give your brain a break from the incessant input. Even a day can have a positive impact.

Be Grateful

Write down three things that make you grateful. They don't have to be big things, and frankly, it's better if they aren't. If you can be grateful for very small things, you get to be grateful a much greater percentage of the time than if it takes a fabulous vacation or a new car to get that feeling. I've seen it suggested in many places that you should write down three things every day. But even if you only do it occasionally, there's still great benefit to you.

Share Your Time

Volunteering takes your mind off yourself—which is a good thing. You can volunteer at a local organization that matters to you. Volunteering to help an overwhelmed co-worker counts, too. Volunteering in any capacity is good for your spirit. Goodness and generosity have a way of spreading.

You Time

During stressful times it can be difficult to think of anything that's going to help your mood or mindset—outside of chucking your job and becoming a bartender on the beach. You can set yourself up to know just what to do when you're at your wit's end.

Here's how:

Take 10 minutes and jot down activities that make you happy or relaxed. They don't have to be traditionally fun things—simply things that give you a mental lift.

Make a list and alongside each, note how much time it takes for the happy/contented feeling to kick in.

Here are some ideas

- Calling a friend–10 minutes
- Reading–30 minutes
- Going for a run–30 minutes
- Gardening–20 minutes
- Puttering in the garage–1 hour
- Playing a pick-up game with friends–1 hour
- Walking the dog–30 minutes
- Getting a massage–1 hour
- Golf or your favorite sport–2-6 hours
- Cooking/Baking/Barbecuing–90 minutes
- Sharing a good bottle of wine–1 hour-ish
- Cleaning out a drawer–30 minutes
- Ironing–30 minutes (Seriously–I have a client who said this.)
- Browsing through a bookstore–30 minutes
- Watching a movie–2 hours
- Watching Ted Talks or videos on YouTube–10 minutes

When you're at the end of your rope, decide how much time you can spare and turn to your list. If you can, do some of these favorite things *before* you're losing your mind to head off stress before it gets you.

In Closing

In the Introduction, I described common stresses and challenges I see that inspired me to write this book. Now that you've reached the end and completed the work, here is what lies ahead.

You now know what's important to you at your very core, and that insight guides the many decisions you make about how you spend your time.

You start each day rested, with a sense of clarity and purpose. You consistently have a level of comfort about what you do and when you do it.

Your day is filled with moments of striving and contentment and even occasionally a bit of joy. But panic and anxiety are infrequent, and complacence has no place in your life.

As your workday wraps up you're confident in the knowledge that the effort you put forth was your best for that day.

Driving home, instead of being distracted and stressed thinking about everything you didn't get done, you settle in for the drive ready to relax and unwind.

At home, you focus on friends, family, and pastimes. This time for yourself restores your energy and adds fulfillment to life that goes beyond what you do for a living.

You have the mindset and skills to be content with how you spend your time. You know that when you make your minutes matter, everything else takes care of itself.

The minutes you lived today are in the past. But that's okay with you because you made the most of them. And you know how to do it all again tomorrow.

Acknowledgments

There are many, many people who have helped in large and small ways not only on this book but in making my business a success. Even the very small instances of help have had an enormous impact. If you're surprised to see your name here, know that though you may not have realized it at the time, your words, advice or insights have made a huge difference.

Cathy Davis, Jack Davis, Pam Wilson, Maria Rodgers-O'Rourke and Julie Hohe—you are an incredible team. This never would have become a reality without you. Adrienne Luther, you got me instantly and nailed my branding. You are going places, for sure.

Kathy Broska, Marsia Geldert-Murphey, Mark LeBlanc and Nancy Nix-Rice, you unequivocally assured me I could write a book. You're so wise in so many ways I just had to believe you were right.

To the many people who have and continue to share keen insight, valuable advice or helped me get unstuck, thank you. I've never forgotten and work to pay it forward every day. To name some (I'm sure I'm forgetting some, too): Ron Ameln, Shelly Azar, Roger Bielicke, Tim Brownson, Denslow Brown, Roni Chambers, Jim Cornbleet, Cynthia Correll, Dan Coughlin, Eric Currie, Manley Feinberg II, Dale Furtwengler, Craig Hall, Heidi Harris, Lisa Hautly, Russ Henneberry, Tiffany Hoeckelman, Jonathan

Jones, Mary Kausch, Matthew Kimberley, Sue Mace, Gina March, Ali Merchant, Lisa Oxenhandler, Bill Prenatt, Shelley Row, Tom Ruwitch, and Tom Winninger.

If you are now or have ever been a client and are reading this, my deep and sincere gratitude for trusting me to work with you. In every single case you've taught me as well—a bonus that makes my life richer every day.

To subscribers of the Minute Shift, I'm grateful beyond measure that you take the time to read what I send and occasionally let me know how those words impact you.

To Charlie and Doris, you've made me feel like your daughter from day one. I truly hit the parents-in-law jackpot when I married Steve. Your words of encouragement about my business and this book are a precious gift.

To my smart, funny, talented and generous brothers and sister, Kevin, Kathy, Patrick and Christopher, there are no better siblings. It's the remarkable things you've built, accomplished and survived, that inspire me to keep up.

Steve, always being in my corner and supporting me during those frustrating, uncertain times means more than you can fathom. Nick, your sense of purpose, dedication, thoughtfulness and work ethic are an inspiration. You always have been and always will be the best part of my day. If there were no other success in life than us finding you, that would be more than enough.

Made in the USA
Monee, IL
15 September 2022